The Magic of Communication Styles

Understanding Yourself and Those Around You

THE MAGIC OF COMMUNICATION STYLES
Copyright © 2016 by Paul Endress. All rights reserved.

Cardinal House Press
4800 Linglestown Rd.
Suite 302
Harrisburg, PA 17112
www.cardinalhousepress.com

FIRST EDITION

ISBN: 978-0692645666

To Karen and Lisa

The ones I love and who have put up with my experiments all these years.

HERE'S WHAT'S INSIDE

Let The Magic Begin!

Welcome to *The Magic of Communication Styles!*

In these pages you will find an easy-to-understand and easy-to-use framework for understanding your natural communication tendencies and the tendencies of everyone around you—and for getting the best from every communication situation.

As you read, you will quickly begin to recognize patterns in yourself and others that have always been there but you may not have noticed before.

If you are a Big Picture/Action person or just want to "get to the point," you can find a one page summary of this entire book on the last page!

Even before, you will be able to quickly apply what you learn to get fast results.

If you are a person who prefers getting the "big picture" or an overview, just skim though the book and find the call outs like the one on this page. They're easy to find and digest. You can always dig in deeper for more details when you want them.

On the other hand, if you are the type of person who is more interested in details, read on. Contained in these pages are the results of years of study, research, experimentation, and working with tens of thousands of people in seminars and workshops and it's all here for you.

Whichever way you prefer to approach it, it's here for you!

IS IT REALLY MAGIC?

When I told my friends that I was going to write a book, the first question from most of them was "what's the title?"

When I told them that I was going to name it *The Magic of Communication Styles*, many of them thought that magic was the wrong word to use. Could it really be "magic? "

Could there really be mysterious or supernatural forces that influence or control the way that we communicate with other people?

Of course not.

But the word magic can also be defined as something wonderful or exciting. And while magic is mysterious to the untrained, once the secret is exposed everyone can understand how it's done. It becomes obvious and loses its magical properties.

That's what will happen as you read this book.

If you are already an outstanding communicator, you will find many ideas and strategies that you can use to become even better. If you are struggling with your communication (and most people are) there is real magic in this book.

Not "tricks" that involve deception, but rather easy-to-use methods that, with a little practice, will give you the skills you need to transform every conversation.

HOW I GOT HERE

I've always been a good public speaker, but that's not the same as being a good communicator.

When I was in high school I was on the debate team. There's even a full-page picture of me in my yearbook, speaking at a debate platform. But there's a big difference between speaking from a platform and being effective at one-on-one interpersonal communication.

Unfortunately, when it came time for close-up one-on-one interactions, I was just as bad as most people. Maybe worse. And, like most people, I didn't know it. But I thought I was pretty good, because I could speak in public. This false sense of competence made me even worse because I thought I didn't have anything to learn.

The only problem was that reality was quite different. Even though I *thought* I was a good communicator, I wasn't getting the results I wanted and sometimes things would go horribly wrong very quickly.

Because I thought I knew what I was doing when it came to communication, I would blame other people for these problems and failures. I would say that it was their fault that they didn't understand me — it couldn't possibly be mine. After all, I was an accomplished member of the debate team.

It took me years, but I finally realized that the true fault for my problems lay with me, not them. **If people weren't understanding me, it was my fault, not theirs**.

This discovery is so important that I'm going to invest pages of this book in discussing it with you and making sure that you make this crucial mental change for yourself. It's one thing that you can change in seconds and get the benefits for the rest of your life.

When I say that I "eventually" realized that my problems were of my own making and not the fault of others, I really mean quite a bit later in my life, about fifteen years ago. That was the time I experienced one of those life events when significant, even fundamental change occurs, but we don't necessarily realize that fact at the time.

Years later, we can look back on that moment and clearly see its importance in our lives. For me, this occurred in December of 1999, when I went to an event hosted by thought leader and personal change expert Tony Robbins.

TWENTY FEET OF BURNING COALS

If you've never gone to a Tony Robbins event, you need to go. For me, the transformational part of the weekend was a "fire walk" on Friday night where we took off our shoes and socks and walked on 20 feet of burning coals without getting hurt.

That walk fascinated me. Obviously it had happened, but I couldn't understand how it was possible. How could I—all of us, really—walk across those hot coals without burning our feet? We did something I would never have believed anyone could do. But we all did.

As the weekend went on, Tony worked with dozens of people to help them implement changes in their personal or business lives. The strategies that he used worked even when these were problems they'd had for five, ten, or even twenty years. He was able to help them to make changes and solve lifelong problems in a very short period of time, sometimes in only 20 or 30 minutes.

After that weekend event I decided that I had to know how this was done so I started to study psychology, but not general psychology like someone would learn in a university. Because I was so impressed with what I saw at the live event, I chose the same branch of psychology that Tony used.

These methods are in general called Ericksonian psychology with much of the later research done by Richard Bandler. The distinction about this type of psychology is that the methodology of research is not to put rats in a lab, or to survey people, or to conduct behavioral experiments.

The Ericksonian method is based on finding people who are good at something, modeling them to find out what makes them good, and then using that model as the basis for changing behavior or for teaching. This modeling approach works not only in learning good behavior, but in un-learning bad behaviors. And it frequently works much more quickly than people expect.

If an Ericksonian wants to solve a problem, he or she will look for people who used to have a problem, but no longer have it. Next, they'll find out what these individuals did to get rid of their problem. Then they'll use that model as the basis for change. Both of these modeling approaches are the basis for the technology behind the *Communication Styles 2.0* model you will learn later in this book.

Once I got started I was fascinated, so I continued by studying neuroscience, neurolinguistic programming, hypnosis, strategic intervention, and other techniques that were related to solving problems and being an effective communicator. I was quickly rewarded by seeing changes in myself and in other people.

At first, my goal was simply to improve my own skills in order to improve the results from my own business and personal relationships. I wasn't necessarily intending to help other people, or to make big changes in my life or anyone else's. I just wanted to become a better communicator and get the best possible results from every interaction.

I wanted to know what to do when somebody comes into your office screaming at you.

I wanted to know how to help people to buy my products and adopt my ideas.

I wanted to know the best way to help my wife understand how much I love her.

I wanted to know how to get my daughter to clean up her room, and so much more.

The idea behind all of this was to become an expert in the art and science of communication—and I did.

As I became more confident with my new skills I began practicing what I was learning by experimenting on everyone around me. I practiced with my employees. And since my career includes starting nine different companies, I've had the opportunity to practice with hundreds of employees.

I also practiced with our vendors. I even practiced with my family (they let me know when to stop). Basically, everybody I met became an experiment in interpersonal communications. I found out what worked and what didn't work and now I've developed my own methods and techniques.

Gradually, I started teaching others, consulting, and coaching. I've had thousands of people leave my seminars excited about the future and I've seen amazing changes in people I've worked with one-on-one. So I know from experience that what I'm going to share with you works.

IS EVERYONE THE SAME?

Here's a question that will reveal how universal these skills truly are: Is getting a four-year-old to clean up his room the same thing as getting a 40-year-old CEO to give you a raise?

The good news is that the answer is "yes!"

Of course there are difference because of the ages, but the same communication techniques, once you learn them, can be applied to almost any person in any situation.

And the good news is that **once these skills are learned, you'll never forget them.**

LET'S LAY A STRONG FOUNDATION

So, what's the best way to share my discoveries with you?

After teaching thousands of people in my seminars, I know what works and what doesn't work. And just as importantly, I know what people are likely to actually put to use and how to encourage them to do so.

I've eliminated anything that sounds good in theory but is too complicated or takes too much practice to actually integrate into their lives. No "fluff" here, just good actionable strategies that you can put to use and get results right away.

JOIN THE REVOLUTION

For teaching purposes, I've distilled the best of my fifteen years of research and teaching into a set of four practical principles which I call "The Communication Revolution," a system that will create a revolutionary change in your communication.

The second principle of this Revolution, "Understand Yourself and Those Around You," is the subject of the book you are now reading and we'll explore it in depth.

However, in order to get the most out of what you are going to learn in this book, I need to introduce you to the Revolution's first principle—Step Up, Not Down.

STEP UP, NOT DOWN

Principle #1 of the Revolution is an invitation to step up, not down.

It can be implemented in less than a minute because it's a change in attitude, not a technique or strategy that needs to be practiced.

It's easy to blame communication (and other) problems on someone else like I did, but what would happen if you took responsibility for the outcome every time you communicated (or tried to communicate) with someone?

It will give you dramatic improvement quickly. And I'll prove it to you right now.

I'LL STEP UP RIGHT NOW

Let's begin with this example: if you, as a reader, don't understand what I have to say in this book, whose fault is it?

Is it yours because you're not intelligent enough, didn't try hard enough, or got distracted and missed something?

Or is it mine because I haven't written it in an engaging way that you can easily understand and put to use?

Of course it's easier to blame you, but we'll both get better results if I take responsibility for the outcome of the book even though I am communicating with tens (or hundreds) of thousands of people all with different education levels, backgrounds, and natural communication preferences.

> *The result of the communication is the responsibility of the communicator.*

If I assume it's your responsibility, I'm going to have many more problems communicating with you and other people than if I work hard to write my ideas in a way that makes them easier for most people to understand.

It may temporarily feel better to put the responsibility for poor communication on others, but the results will never improve because this "solution" assumes that there's nothing the communicator needs to do to improve anything.

If you put the responsibility on other people, you're creating a system in which nothing really changes and failures continue. Basically, you're turning yourself into a helpless victim—and that's not a recipe for success.

We all know what it feels like to try to communicate something important and to fail.

It feels terrible and it's only natural to believe that terrible feeling is the result of something beyond our control. It's easy to feel like a victim, but in these situations we're a victim of our own actions, or inaction, not someone else's.

I'm challenging you to step up and put the responsibility on yourself.

Learn what works and what doesn't work. And even if you don't consciously change any of your techniques or strategies, when you accept responsibility for the outcome of every communication you will change the way you communicate at an unconscious level. Your unconscious mind will step up and make subtle changes of which you might not even be aware.

Making this simple mental change will be powerful. You're going to seek out and study new strategies, such as this book, so that you can become a better communicator. You'll start to take different actions and communicate in different ways that are going to be more effective—and you'll feel great because success feels a lot better than failure or mediocrity.

CELL PHONES OFF!

A few years ago I decided to implement this first Revolutionary principle for myself—I changed the way I began my workshops.

I used to start out every seminar by saying, "Okay, everybody, put away your cell phones. If there are any cell phones out, we're going to call you out and embarrass you in front of the group." I've even seen some workshop leaders who charge people a dollar for having a cell phone out. It's a really bad way of getting people to turn off their phones, but they did it because they didn't know what else to do.

Instead, I decided to *step up*, apply this first principle to myself, and use it to make my workshops better. I committed myself to being good enough so that if somebody's cell phone rang, they would keep listening to me and ignore their phone. A big challenge, wasn't it?

In order to do that, I had to implement a process of continuous improvement, constantly taking steps to engage the participants, ensuring they didn't want to miss anything by paying attention to their phone. I had to increase the quality of my programs in order to make every piece of content interesting enough to command that kind of attention.

Instead of putting the responsibility on others to adapt themselves to however I delivered my material, I adapted myself to them, even though most people would assume that asking people to turn off their cell phones was a perfectly legitimate request. I forced myself to increase the quality with which I was running my seminars and it dramatically increased the results people got and the amount of positive feedback I got in the form of unsolicited testimonials.

While it may seem to be easier to put the responsibility of communication on others, the results from this approach will never be as good as if you accept this responsibility for yourself. In my workshop example, I would be admitting that my content and presentation weren't as interesting or at least as compelling as a ringing cell phone or an incoming text message.

You can't control what others are going to do, but you can always control what you do.

Even more importantly, believing in yourself by taking on this responsibility moves you to a position of control.

You can't control what other people are going to do, but you can always control what you are going to do. This puts you in a position to change things for the better because you honestly believe that you're the only one responsible for improving your communications. This may seem like a tough challenge, but it's really very good news.

You'll observe situations in a new way and understand that listeners are reacting to you. If they don't respond in the way you want, all you need to do is adjust something you can control—your own actions and Communication Style— rather than being frustrated by them "not getting it."

Simply deciding to *step up* (putting the responsibility onto yourself), not down (allowing yourself to be the victim of other people's behavior) will have an immediate impact on your results in every communication situation.
It's truly the one thing that changes everything.

PRACTICAL RESULTS

The practical side of this principle is that once you accept communication responsibility, you're going to work to adapt yourself to others rather than expecting them to adapt to you. This leads us to Communication Revolution Principle #2 and the subject of this book.

UNDERSTAND YOURSELF AND THOSE AROUND YOU

This principle is easy to understand and simple to implement. The only downside is that it takes a little more work in the short term, but the upside is that it will **improve your communication results for the rest of your life**.

In much of the time we spend with people, we tend to do what comes naturally. In other words, when it comes to communicating, we express ideas using our own natural Communication Style.

This makes the success or failure of our communication seem random because we don't really know in advance what we're going to do naturally. We just do it. That may be good advice when it comes to exercising, but it's not the way to develop outstanding (or even above average) communication skills.

Without some study, practice, and paying attention to what we are doing we're likely just to blurt out whatever comes to mind and then success or failure becomes a matter of good or bad luck. And luck isn't a very good way to ensure better relationships and more of what you want out of life.

You know from experience that we are likely to succeed more frequently when among friends who know us well enough so that we've already created a favorable environment for successful communication. You know the situations I'm talking about—you can each predict almost exactly what the other will do or say before you do or say it.

We're most likely to be challenged in situations when we're talking to someone new, communicating with people we know well but have developed bad patterns with over the years, or when using email.

In these cases, not only don't we plan what we're going to do or say in advance and how the other person is likely to respond when we simply do "what comes naturally," but (especially with email) we also won't have any idea about how our listeners or readers are going to interpret our communication.

They're most likely going to respond by doing "what comes naturally" to them and, unless we are lucky, we don't have a very good chance of success.

Now is the time to *step up*, take responsibility, and take action!

Let's invest a few hours together right now to learn a few easy but powerful concepts and strategies that eliminate luck and replace it with skills that will give you outstanding results for the rest of your life.

In what situations have you been frustrated or disappointed with the outcome of your communication?
How could you *step up* and take responsibility for this situation?

WELCOME TO *COMMUNICATION STYLES 2.0*

SO...WHAT IS A COMMUNICATION STYLE?

For most of my life, I assumed (if I thought about it at all) that other people were just like me. Of course this was a bad assumption, but I was never taught the natural differences in Communication Styles between different people. I was getting generally bad results because I was relying on luck for success—and as we said before, this is not a winning strategy.

When we assume that other people are just like us, we tend to communicate in the style that we like to be talked to and we overlay our interpretation of events and social situations onto other people's communication.

As we discussed in the last chapter, doing what comes naturally is not a reliable recipe for success in communicating, which is why I recommend stepping up, taking responsibility, understanding the preferences of other people, and adapting our behavior and Communication Style to other people's preferences. It turns luck into skill which is a much more reliable strategy for communication success.

HERE'S THE DEFINITION

Let's take a moment to define the term, "Communication Style." It is a person's regular or familiar communication

A Communication Style is a person's communication patterns and preferences that they use in a wide variety of situations.

patterns and the strategies they use to communicate across a broad variety of situations. In other words, it's how we relate to others.

Here are some quick facts about Communication Styles:

- Everybody (whether they know what it is or not) has a natural Communication Style that he or she uses without thinking.
- You can achieve the best results by adapting your style to the style of the other person(s).
- When you adapt to another person it takes energy because you are doing something that is not natural for you.
- If we're forced to adapt for an extended period, we eventually run out of energy and revert to our natural style.
- Under stress we tend to revert to our natural Communication Style.

Another characteristic of Communication Styles is that we communicate most easily with people who are most like us or, put another way, those individuals who have a Communication Style that is similar to ours. Conversely, it's most difficult for us to communicate with those who are not like us and have dramatically different Communication Styles.

It's also important to know that Communication Styles are situational. When you think about it, you'll realize that you instinctively adapt your Communication Style depending on where you are or who you're talking to.

When we're with friends or family, we probably behave and talk differently than we do at work. When we want to convey something important to someone in any situation—

at work or in social situation—we make conscious efforts to adapt and do what will work best in that situation.

While we all have a natural Communication Style that we use without thinking, we also adapt our style as necessary. Here are three common types of adaptations that you will recognize from your own experience.

ROLE ADAPTATIONS

The first category is one I call "role adaptation." In our lives, and even during a typical day, we each play many "roles."

An example might be the role of wife compared to the role of mother. Another might be the role of boss compared to the role of husband or father. In each of these cases we will quite naturally behave and communicate differently based upon the role we are in at the time.

There are obvious practical reasons for this. The way we communicate at work may give us terrible results at home, and vice versa. Giving orders might be effective at a construction site, but it probably won't work as well at home.

Of course, some people don't make changes in order to adapt to different situations, but most people have learned from experience to modify their Communication Style for different roles, at least on some level.

The specific ways that we adapt to different roles will not always be the same for everyone; there are people who are more relaxed in their work role than with family and friends. Our job may be easy and familiar for us, while our family members may require us to expend a lot of energy to get along with them.

Since our natural Communication Style requires us to expend the least amount of energy, one good way to tell whether we are using our natural style with someone is to answer the question, "does this make me tired?"

If you are using a style that comes naturally to you and not using an energy-expending role adaptation, it will require less energy and you will be less tired.

FAVORABLE OR UNFAVORABLE ENVIRONMENT

A second common adaptation of our Communication Style is based on whether we believe we are in a favorable or unfavorable environment.

When we're in comfortable situations with people we know and trust, we tend to communicate in different ways than we do when we're in situations that are unfamiliar, or which we may perceive as being dangerous.

This is different than role-based adaptation in that a role adaptation is based upon who we are with and an environmental adaptation is based on where we are.

SITUATIONS THAT MAY BE STRESSFUL OR NOT

The third adaptation is based on whether the situation is stressful or not because, as we noted before, during stressful times we tend to revert to our natural Communication Style.

Stress can simply be the result of being tired, even if we are happily at a party or social gathering or just reaching the end of a long day at work. Stress can also be a completely internal reaction and does not have to be the result of any social situation.

One thing to notice in each of these three adaptations—stress, an unfamiliar environment, or the need for role adaptation—is that they can cause either conscious or unconscious adjustments in the way we communicate.

For example, we can decide to adapt our style in order to accomplish a goal at work or at home, or we can take extra caution when we sense we're in an unfavorable situation, or we can opt not to get into a serious conversation when we know we're tired and might not be able to focus on things.

Most of our adaptations are unconscious and happen so fast that we don't even realize that we are doing them.

NEXT...

Now that we've laid the foundation, it's time to learn the *Communication Styles 2.0* model and how to put it to use.

Let's go!

The Two Dimensions of Communication

After years of research, conducting seminars, and working with tens of thousands of people, I've created the *Communication Styles 2.0* model and *Circle of Styles*.

These two tools make it easy for you to understand your natural communication tendencies and see how you are likely to interact with others with either similar or completely different natural tendencies.

Best of all, these concepts are easy to understand, easy to use, and will benefit you for the rest of your life.

THE TWO DIMENSIONS

1. Everyone has a natural Communication Style which is a person's regular or familiar communication patterns and the strategies they use to communicate across a broad variety of situations. It's how we relate to others.

2. There are two dimensions of communication and everyone falls somewhere on these two axis.

3. To be a successful communicator, understand where you fall on each of the axis and where the other person falls. Be aware of your natural tendencies and adapt them to match the style of the other person.

Let's explore the first dimension of communication.

TASK VS. PEOPLE

The first axis of communication is the horizontal axis and it symbolically represents a tendency to focus on the task compared to a tendency to focus on people and relationships when communicating.

It can be represented as a line like this:

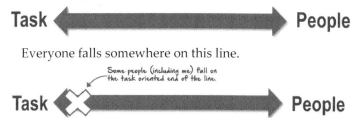

Everyone falls somewhere on this line.

Those of us who fall on the far left of the line have a very strong tendency to be task oriented, focusing on "getting to the point" and getting things done when we are talking with someone.

Some people fall toward right end of the line and tend to focus on building and maintaining relationships when they are communicating and interacting with other people.

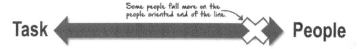

When I explain this as part of a workshop, I usually get questions related to which one is better or which one is right or wrong. Here's the answer as clearly as I can say it: **Neither of these is right or wrong, neither is better or worse than the other. They just are what they are.**

IN REAL LIFE

Even though neither is better than the other, could there be a built-in natural conflict between the natural

Communication Style of someone who is people oriented and someone who is task oriented?

When they get together with someone for a meeting or a conversation, the task oriented person is likely to want to get right to the point because many times they might see the "people stuff" as a waste of time that just slows everything down and doesn't contribute to the completion of the task at hand.

This doesn't mean that the task oriented person doesn't like people and that they aren't good at interpersonal interactions, it just means that their natural tendency is to focus on the task rather than the people and relationship aspects of the communication.

On the other hand, the person with the people orientation sees the relationship as an important part of the communication and a critical part of accomplishing the task. They can be surprised and possibly offended by someone who just wants to get right to the point and accomplish the task.

The farther two people are from each other on the task/people axis, the more likely they are to have challenges when communicating unless they expend the energy required to understand and adapt to each other.

Later on in this chapter I'll give you more details about this built-in conflict and some proven strategies for turning it to the advantage of everyone involved.

But not everyone is on one end of the line or the other.

THE REALITY

In practice, most people fall somewhere along the axis rather than at one end or the other.

In this illustration, because this person is past the middle point and still on the people side of the line, they have a people tendency in their communication but less so than someone who is all the way to the right end of the line.

These people who are more toward the middle of the line are interested in task completion more than someone who is all the way to the right. Because they are more toward the middle, they will communicate differently than someone who is far to the right and is completely people oriented.

The person who is on the far right may have many great relationships but have trouble completing projects, whereas this person who is more in the middle will tend to both take action *and* build relationships.

In this example, because they are more to the people side of the line, this person will tend to choose people over task. In a work situation this might mean that they don't want to confront a subordinate about an assignment that is behind schedule because they don't want to risk the relationship.

On the other hand, someone who is on the task end of the line may inadvertently destroy a relationship in the interest of completing a task. And that might not matter to them.

The farther to the left they are on the line, the stronger their task tendency in communication. The farther to the right they are on the line, the stronger their people orientation. By knowing where you and/or someone else falls on the line you can accurately predict how you will communicate using your natural Communication Styles. Remember—neither is right or wrong, better or worse.

FINDING YOUR PLACE ON THE AXIS

There are two ways to find your location on the axis:

1. Use our online survey
2. Estimate your position yourself

USING OUR ONLINE ASSESSMENT

The most accurate and detailed way to find out not only where you fall on the task/people axis but your entire Communication Style and your exact position on the *Communication Styles 2.0 Circle of Styles* is to use our online survey.

It takes less than ten minutes to complete and gives you a comprehensive twenty-five page report that explains your tendencies, strengths, challenges, and gives you an action plan and a grid that shows how to be most effective with each of the other styles.

I'll explain all about the twenty-one Communication Styles in the next chapter.

If you received a link or code to access the online survey with this book, go ahead and use it now. If you don't have one and want to purchase one, you can do so at:

www.communicationstyles2.com/survey

If you don't have a link, don't want to purchase one, or simply don't want to take the survey right now, you can use the estimation method below.

Estimating won't give you as accurate of a result as using the online survey, but it will get you started.

ESTIMATING YOUR POSITION

Estimating your position on the line is easy to do. Simply mark where you think you fall on the line below.

Even though we've been programmed our entire lives that higher numbers are better than lower numbers, in this case 10 isn't better than 1.

There are no right or wrong numbers, so go ahead and estimate your position right now. Place an X on the line where you think you fall between the task and people orientations.

NATURAL TENDENCIES

Here are a few of the tendencies of communicators on each end of the axis.

The Task Oriented Communicator	The People Oriented Communicator
• Direct communication	• Outgoing
• Can be overbearing	• Persuasive
• Pragmatic	• Might have time management challenges
• Likes competition	
• Can overlook details	• Can be overdramatic
• May be a poor listener	• Considers others feelings

Next, we'll take a look at the vertical axis and then learn some of the natural behaviors of the Styles, how to find someone else's Style, and how to adapt quickly to others.

BIG PICTURE VS. DETAILS

The second axis of communication is the vertical axis and it symbolically represents a tendency to focus on the big picture compared to a tendency to focus on details when communicating.

Once again, everyone falls somewhere along the line between the two extremes. I fall on the upper end of the line right near the top at the big picture arrow.

This means that my natural tendency when communicating is to focus on the big picture at the expense of the details.

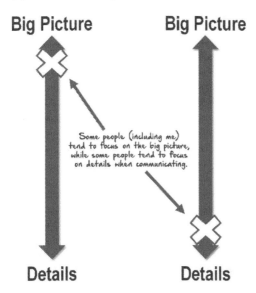

Some people (including me) tend to focus on the big picture, while some people tend to focus on details when communicating.

What kind of problems or challenges could this tendency cause for me?

REALITY AGAIN

Just like the task/people line, most people don't fall on the extremes like I do.

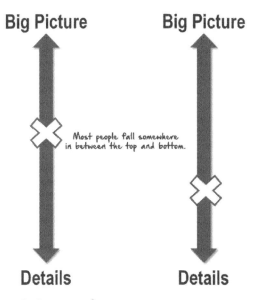

COULD THERE BE PROBLEMS?

As you can imagine, someone who has a natural tendency to focus on the big picture and has not much interest in details could easily irritate a detail oriented communicator.

Of course, the opposite is also true. The detail person could really annoy the big picture person with their questions and insistence on knowing the exact who, what, when, where, and why of a situation, assignment, or story.

A big picture person will say "let's go on vacation." And the detail person will respond with "where will we stay?" or "how long?" or "how will we pay for it?" or maybe even "what if it rains?" Unfortunately, the big picture person has thought about none of these things and is simply thinking about the big idea of "going on vacation."

You can see the potential for conflict and miscommunication if each person only uses his or her natural tendencies.

Once again, neither is better than the other or right or wrong. They simply are what they are. But they can sure irritate each other if they're not aware of each other's tendencies and careful in their communication.

NATURAL TENDENCIES

Here are a few of tendencies of communicators on each end of the axis.

The Big Picture Oriented Communicator	The Detail Oriented Communicator
• Usually looks at the positive side of things	• Analytical
• Expects things to "work out"	• Spots potential problems
• Talks in terms of generalities	• Stays calm and rational
• Might miss potential problems	• Excels at problem solving
	• Likely to have questions

ESTIMATING YOUR POSITION

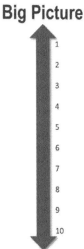

Big Picture

1
2
3
4
5
6
7
8
9
10

If you don't have access to the online survey, just use this illustration to estimate your position. Estimating your position on the line is easy to do. Simply mark where you think you fall on the vertical big picture/details line.

Details

WHAT ABOUT NATURAL CONFLICT?

The two dimensions of the *Communication Styles 2.0* model give you a clear way to predict how easy or difficult it will be to communicate with someone using your natural style.

The closer you are to someone on one of the axis, the easier it will be to communicate with them using your natural style.

The farther away you are, the more natural conflict and misunderstandings are likely to occur, but it's not inevitable. This is especially true now that you understand your own tendencies.

It's important to realize that there is value in having people with different communication styles interacting and working with each other. The big picture person can benefit from the tendencies of the detail person and vice versa. The world would be a boring place if everyone were the same.

YOU MIGHT NEED TO STEP UP

As I mentioned in the previous chapter, the first principle of the Communication Revolution is to "step up" and take responsibility for the outcome of your communication and this is the perfect place to put that principle into practice.

Take responsibility for adapting your natural style to the needs of the other person. If you are big picture, force yourself to pay attention to the details and don't let yourself get irritated if someone asks you a lot of questions. If you are detail oriented be prepared with a summary when you engage the big picture person.

If you're task oriented and working with a people oriented communicator, take the time to invest in the relationship that is so important to the other person. If you are people oriented and need to communicate with a task person, just skip the small talk and get to the point.

A little bit of effort on your part will go a long way toward making you an expert communicator who can work with a wide variety of styles whether they are similar to you or not.

Remember…you can't control what the other person does, but you can always control what you do.

HOW TO CONTROL YOUR EMOTIONS

If you find yourself getting angry, irritated, frustrated, or any other negative emotion when you have to communicate with someone who has a natural style that is different than yours, here's a question you can use to find the meaning you are assigning that is causing you to feel the way you do.

This is especially necessary if you are convinced that the other person is doing what they are doing on purpose to irritate you. It is possible (but not likely) that they are doing it on purpose, but letting them control you won't benefit either of you.

Emotions are the result of the meaning that you assign to an event, not the event itself. Think about the problem situation and examine what meaning you are assigning to the events. Then ask yourself this question to discover other possible meanings: What else could this mean?

PUTTING THE TWO AXIS TOGETHER

In the *Communication Styles 2.0* model, the two axis intersect with each other like this:

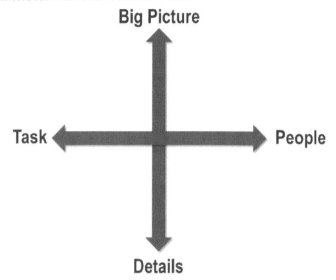

By combining your position on the big picture/detail axis with your position on the task/people axis you can find out where the two intersect and this will lead you to your specific style.

I know that the detail communicators reading this will be concerned about getting their position as exact as possible, and that's an important and useful trait. For those people, I'm going to suggest that for the purpose of what we are doing here, close is good enough. Do your best, and you can always come back and refine it later after you learn more.

If you used the online survey, your location has already been plotted exactly for you using our algorithm.

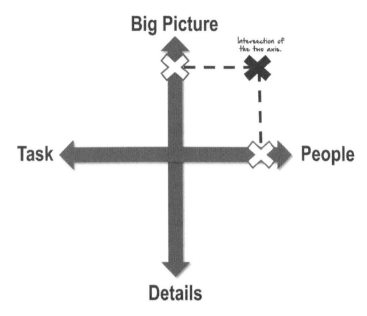

In this illustration, I have plotted the intersection of positions on each of the two axis. If you are using the manual estimation method to find your Communication Style, you can see how to extrapolate where the two will intersect and use this to find your position on the *Communication Styles 2.0 Circle of Styles*.

THE COMMUNICATION STYLES 2.0 CIRCLE OF STYLES

The next step is to give the Communication Styles names by overlaying the *Circle of Styles* onto the two axis. Here's the result:

Big Picture

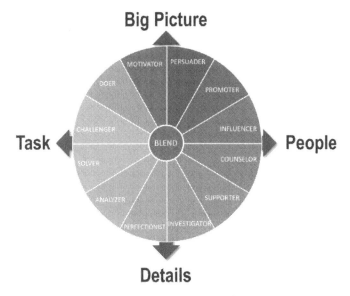

Task ◄ ► **People**

Details

This version of the *Communication Styles 2.0* model *Circle of Styles* shows only the twelve primary Communication Styles. There are nine more Styles that are combinations of these basic twelve, but right now we are going to concentrate on understanding the basic twelve and their motivations.

HOW TO USE THE *CIRCLE OF STYLES*

Because the *Circle of Styles* overlays the two axis, it is easy to determine the basic characteristics of each of the Styles based upon their location on the *Circle*.

The six Styles on the left side of the *Circle* tend to be task oriented in their communication and the six Styles on the right side tend to be people oriented when they communicate.

Likewise, the six on the top tend to be big picture and the six on the bottom are oriented more toward details when they talk to or email you.

PREDICTING CONFLICT

Using the *Communication Styles 2.0* model *Circle of Styles* to predict conflict is straightforward. Those styles directly across from each other on the *Circle* are likely to be in conflict if they use their natural tendencies when communicating with each other.

A useful exercise is to mark the positions of multiple people on the *Circle* to see how they will interact with each other. Those closest to each other on the *Circle* will communicate easily using their natural styles. Those farther apart are more likely to have a misunderstanding or conflict.

It's a great tool to create a "team map" and I'll show you exactly how to do it later in this book. Once this map is created, you can easily see opportunities and challenges presented by the natural communication tendencies of each member of the group.

UNDERSTANDING THE TENDENCIES

The Communication Styles with the strongest tendencies are those on the diagonal of the *Circle*.

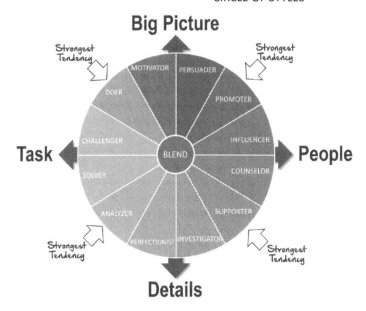

The Doer is the most task/big picture oriented style.

The Promoter is the most big picture/people oriented.

The Supporter is the most people/detail oriented.

The Analyzer is the most detail/task oriented.

As you move around the *Circle* from the diagonals, the tendencies begin to combine and soften. For example, as you move to the right and around the top of the *Circle* from the Doer to the Motivator, the tendency becomes less about task and more about people.

The Persuader is even less task and more people than the Motivator until you arrive at the Promoter who is strongly people oriented in their communication tendencies.

Using this basic knowledge, you can deduce the basic tendencies of any Style on the *Circle*. This gives you an excellent way of quickly understanding how you will interact with any other style.

Is It This Simple?

Sort of.

I know that for some readers (the big picture styles) that's a good enough answer, but for many of you (the detail styles), it's not. So let me give you more insight into the details.

1. This basic *Communication Styles 2.0* model and *Circle of Styles* give you a quick way to understand yourself and anticipate how you will communicate with anyone else on the *Circle* using your natural style. I'll explain more about this soon.

2. The two axis are designed to be simple so that they are fast and easy to understand and use, but people aren't quite this simple. Each of the communication styles have a much greater depth of tendencies, strengths, and weaknesses than the few that I have included here. I'll provide some more details later in the book and you'll be able to read about them in action when we meet the executives of 366 Solar, but the best way to get a deeper level of detail is to use the online survey.

3. Not everyone fits neatly into one of these twelve styles. Some people are combinations of these twelve foundational styles and because of this are called the "blends." This provides more precision and detail and I'll give you a lot more information about the blends in the next chapter when we meet the Styles.

THE MOTIVATIONS

When I started to use the *Communication Styles 2.0* model in seminars, people were amazed by how easy it is to put to use.

But they (especially the big picture communicators) wanted something even easier to use than the twelve styles and the detail communicators wanted even more precision and details.

So for those of you who want more of a big picture, I've grouped the styles together based upon their primary motivation. This is the primary characteristic that drives their communication.

When someone is using their natural Communication Style, you will be able to observe their primary motivation whether they are talking or listening.

While the simplification loses detail, it makes it easier to understand and use.

Here are the four primary motivations and the Styles that are included in each of them. The first Style in each group has the strongest motivation of that type.

Motivation	Styles
Action	Doer, Motivator, Challenger, Chancellor, Attainer
People	Promoter, Persuader, Influencer, Director, Appraiser
Safety	Supporter, Investigator, Counselor, Advocate, Achiever
Order	Analyzer, Perfectionist, Solver, Contemplator, Practitioner

HERE'S THE *CIRCLE OF STYLES* WITH THE MOTIVATIONS

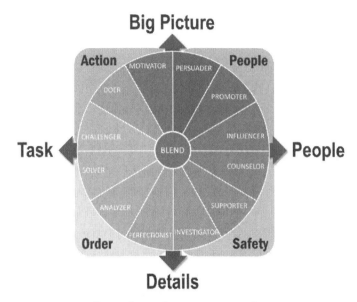

You can easily see how they group together.

Just like the individual Styles, the strongest motivation is on the diagonal so the Doer is the most motivated by action, the Promoter is most motivated by people, the Supporter is most motivated by safety, and the Analyzer is most motivated by order. As you move around the *Circle*, they blend together and moderate.

MOTIVATIONS AND CONFLICT

Knowing the motivations provides a convenient way to think about and predict conflict. Styles directly across from each other on the *Circle* have an inherent level of conflict caused by their conflicting motivations.

In situations where one person is motivated by people and the other person is motivated by order there is likely to be a challenge because people are not orderly and predictable.

When someone is motivated by action and another person is motivated by safety there is also likely to be conflict because taking action can be perceived as risky and make the Safety Style person unwilling to act.

The Action Style person is likely to become frustrated by the natural caution of the Safety Style person because it conflicts with their natural motivation to take action and get things done.

CHALLENGES BETWEEN THE SAME MOTIVATIONS

There can also be challenges (not usually direct conflict) with Styles that have the same motivation communicating with each other.

Styles	Possible Challenge
Two Action Styles	Because both people are motivated by action the conflict won't be about whether to take action or not because they both agree on that. The conflict will be about who is going to control the action.
Two People Styles	When People Styles get together it's not likely that there will be conflict, but they may spend so much time building their relationship that work doesn't get done.
Two Safety Styles	Conflict is unlikely with the Safety Styles. They will generally get along well.
Two Order Styles	If there is conflict between these Styles it will be about details or the meaning of data more than anything else.

THE BLEND STYLES

Because not everyone falls neatly into one of the twelve primary Communication Styles, the *Communication Styles 2.0* model has nine additional Styles to give it extra precision when describing a person's natural Communication Style.

These blended styles each have a primary underlying Communication Style but expand to include characteristics of some of the adjacent Styles.

You will appreciate the subtle distinctions between Communication Styles that these blends make possible. This level of detail is especially valuable when comparing individuals to each other, diagnosing problems, or working with teams.

Because these Styles are combinations of their underlying Styles, I'm not going to go into great detail about each of them. You can come to your own conclusions by understanding the Styles that underlie each blend and drawing the necessary inferences.

If you are using the automated online survey, this will be done for you and the unique characteristics of each person will be revealed in addition to the underlying generalities.

HERE'S AN EXAMPLE

To explain exactly how this works, I'll use the following illustration of the blended Chancellor Style.

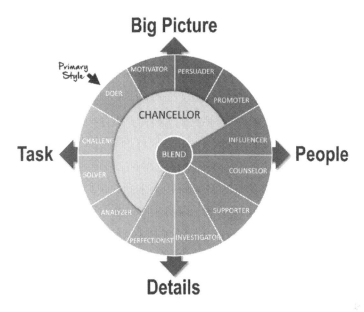

Big Picture

Task

People

Details

In this illustration of the *Communication Styles 2.0 Circle of Styles*, you can see that the Chancellor Style covers the area from Analyzer to Promoter. The center of the arc falls on the Doer.

Because the Doer is at the midpoint of the arc, it is the primary style behind the Chancellor and the Chancellor will mainly have the characteristics and motivations of the Doer.

However, since the Chancellor also wraps around the *Circle* in the direction of the Promoter who is people motivated and the Analyzer who is order motivated, you can know that the natural action motivation of the Doer is modified by the additional motivations of order and people.

As the arc moves farther away from its center point the influence of the underlying Styles decreases. In this Chancellor example, this means that the impact of the Doer is greatest, the Challenger and Motivator are secondary, the Solver and Persuader have the next amount of impact, and the Analyzer and Promoter have the least amount of impact.

The relative levels of impact are unique to each person and are limited only by the underlying technology used to measure them.

THE ULTIMATE BLEND STYLE IS THE BLEND

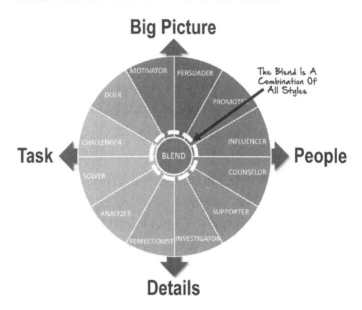

The Blend Style is more or less an equal combination of all of the Styles. This combination is found relatively rarely, but a person whose natural Communication Style is the Blend Style can easily communicate with almost anybody.

If you know anyone who has this Style, you know how easy they are to get along with!

THE DIAGONAL STYLES

THE APPRAISER AND THE PRACTITIONER

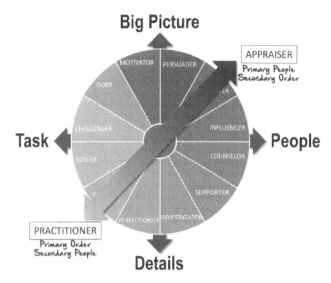

THE ATTAINER AND THE ACHIEVER

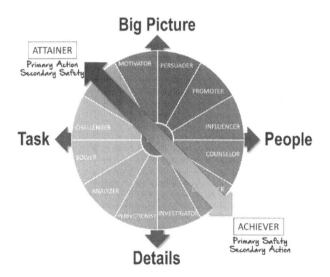

The Appraiser, Practitioner, Attainer, and Achiever are called the diagonal Styles because each one is a blend of two Styles that are not next to each other on the *Circle*, but are opposite each other.

Because the two underlying Styles blended into each of the diagonal Styles are opposite each other on the *Circle*, it creates an internal conflict within the communicator and can cause them to communicate in what appear to be contradictory ways at different times.

Here's exactly how the underlying styles combine to create the diagonal styles.

Communication Style	Dominant Underlying Style	Secondary Underlying Style
Attainer	Doer (Action Motivation)	Supporter (Safety Motivation)
Achiever	Supporter (Safety Motivation)	Doer (Action Motivation)
Appraiser	Promoter (People Motivation)	Analyzer (Order Motivation)
Practitioner	Analyzer (Order Motivation)	Promoter (People Motivation)

As you can imagine, if someone is an Attainer and is primarily motivated by action and has a secondary motivation of safety it will cause them to sometimes communicate in ways that are highly task and action oriented and sometimes back off a communication in a seemingly contradictory style because of safety concerns.

People are endlessly interesting and challenging, and these four Styles are great examples of the diversity you will find as you communicate with a variety of people. Enjoy!

USING COMMUNICATION STYLES WITH TEAMS

So far I've talked only about how to use *Communication Styles 2.0* to understand the Style of one person at a time, but this technology can be used to great benefit with teams and groups of all sizes.

The key is to create a team map like this one I created for the team at 366 Solar:

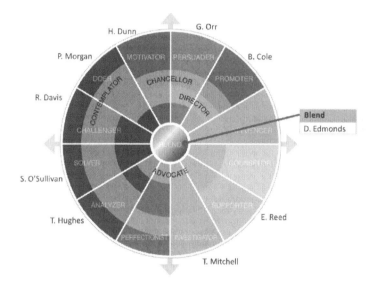

All you have to do is take the names of the team members and place them around the outside of the *Circle* next to their communication style. Then you can look at the map and instantly see who communicates well with each other naturally and where the difficulties are likely to be.

In this example, since Morgan is across from Reed and Mitchell you can readily see there is likely to be a challenge here. Reed and Mitchel will probably communicate easily with each other but will be challenged by the action motivation and task orientation of Morgan.

A MORE COMPLEX MAP

This map includes almost fifty people including many Blend Styles. Now that you understand how the *Communication Styles 2.0* model and *Circle of Styles* work, you can see how effective this can be for understanding even large teams.

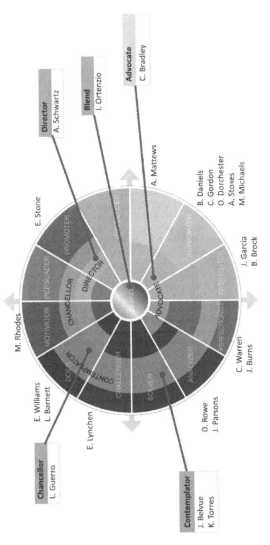

NOW YOU TRY IT

Here's a sample team map:

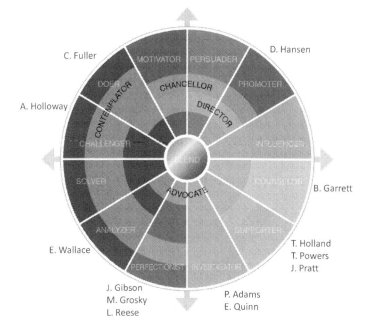

HERE ARE A FEW QUESTIONS

1. Who will Holland, Powers, and Pratt (all Supporters) have trouble communicating with?
2. Who will Hansen (Promoter) be challenged by?
3. Will Gibson, Grosky, and Reese work well together?
4. How about Fuller and Holloway?
5. If you were going to advise Fuller on how to communicate better with Adams, what would your advice be?

MANAGING CONFLICT BETWEEN THE STYLES

By now you have a working understanding of the Communication Styles, their motivations, some of their characteristics, and how people with different styles are likely to communicate with each other.

Now it's time to introduce some strategies that you can use to bring peace and harmony to relationships and help people be more effective with each other when their Communication Styles are not naturally aligned.

IF YOU ARE INVOLVED IN THE CONFLICT

STEP UP

This is by far the best and most effective advice I can give you and it's a repeat of the section in the beginning of the book titled "Step Up, Not Down."

If you are having trouble communicating with someone, I highly recommend that you go back and read that section again. Here's a quick outline of what you should do:

1. Recognize that you can't control what someone else is going to do. Their behavior is partly controlled by their Communication Style, but there are many other influences at work that are outside the scope of this book.
2. Realize that you can control what you do. It may take a lot of energy and it might not be easy, but you can absolutely control what you do in any situation.
3. Resolve to adapt yourself to the other person by changing the way you are communicating to whatever works best with them. This book gives you a powerful set of tools with the *Communication Styles 2.0* model and technology and now is the time to put them to use.

4. Repeat as often as necessary. If what you are doing isn't resolving the problem and getting you the results you want, try something else. Keep experimenting until you find the solution.

5. Remember that it's up to you. Even if the conflict or problem isn't your fault, the only way you can be sure of solving it is to take responsibility, adapt your style as necessary, and keep at it until you succeed.

TAKE ACTION

Sounds obvious and simple, doesn't it?

It is unless you get trapped in a cycle where you are paralyzed by not taking action until you can be sure that what you are planning will work.

Even though *Communication Styles 2.0* provides you with an easy-to-use model for understanding yourself and those around you, people are still endlessly variable and many times unpredictable.

If you don't take action, you guarantee that things will never change. By taking action you can improve your life and the lives of others.

IF YOU ARE NOT INVOLVED IN THE CONFLICT

EDUCATE THE GROUP

Despite my best efforts, most people don't know about the *Communication Styles 2.0* model and how it can help them to understand themselves and the other people with whom they communicate.

Now that you know about the model and *Circle*, share it with the group. You could get them copies of this book, give them access to the online survey which creates a customized action plan for each person, or you could provide them with live or online training.

At the very least, you could tell them what you have learned and guide them to using it to resolve the conflict.

EMPOWER THE GROUP

Give them the education and tools they need to be successful. Most people were never taught how to communicate at home or in school so now is the time to give them what they need to be more effective communicators.

REWARD GOOD BEHAVIOR

Make sure that you give credit and praise when someone does something positive. You might even provide financial incentives for good behavior.

Another good strategy is to create group norms that provide approval for good behavior and disapproval for bad behavior. People will catch on quickly and start behaving better whether they feel like it or not.

Meet The Styles

In this section of the book, I'll introduce you to each of the twelve primary Communication Styles and give you an overview of each of them.

These descriptions aren't intended to be complete, but rather to give you some basic ideas of how each of these styles will communicate.

For ease of understanding, I've grouped them by their primary motivation.

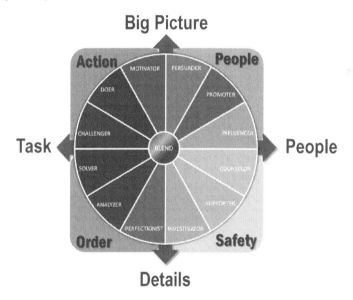

THE ACTION STYLES

The Action Styles are in the upper left section of the *Communication Styles 2.0 Circle of Styles.*

The primary Action Style is the Doer with the Challenger and Motivator also showing a significant Action motivation. The Chancellor and Attainer are blends that feature Action as their primary motivator.

SHARED CHARACTERISTICS OF THE ACTION STYLES

- They tend to be blunt, straightforward, and get right to the point
- Very direct and can be quite forceful when speaking
- Usually convinced they are right so they try to persuade others
- Because they are not easily threatened by criticism they will engage in difficult conversations that others avoid
- They can become impatient with those who are not as task and action oriented
- Can be too transparent with emotions and their emotions can show in body language
- They tend to question authority and speak their mind

THE DOER

The primary interest of a Doer when communicating is to get things done.

Doers are typically people whom others perceive as a very active, independent, self-confident, and results-oriented kind of person. As an extension of this, they may appear to be bossy at times or even disregard other people's feelings when it comes to getting things done.

QUICK SUMMARY AND CROSS-REFERENCE

Primary Motivation	Action
Secondary Motivation	
Most Likely to Have Conflict With	Supporter
Also Likely to Have Conflict With	Investigator, Counselor, Advocate
366 Solar Executives Who Are Doers	Paul Morgan

HOW TO BE MOST EFFECTIVE WITH A DOER

- Get to the point fairly quickly.
- Give them the "big picture" and then be prepared with details if requested.
- If you present a problem, come prepared with a solution.
- Answer the question "What are the benefits?" not "How will we get it done?"

THE MOTIVATOR

The primary interest of a Motivator when communicating is working with people to get things done.

Motivators typically have excellent communication skills and have a strong desire for results which makes them excellent leaders who enjoy getting the best from others. While they seek to get things done, they also make sure to include others in their plans and delegate as much as possible.

QUICK SUMMARY AND CROSS-REFERENCE

Primary Motivation	Action
Secondary Motivation	People
Most Likely to Have Conflict With	Investigator
Also Likely to Have Conflict With	Perfectionist, Supporter, Advocate
366 Solar Executives Who Are Motivators	Howard Dunn

HOW TO BE MOST EFFECTIVE WITH A MOTIVATOR

- Engage them socially, but make sure you get to the point fairly quickly.
- Don't give them many details unless they ask for them.
- Show an interest in them as a person, but you don't need to build a deep relationship.

THE CHALLENGER

The primary interest of a Challenger when communicating is making sure that things get done right.

Challengers are highly action oriented and willing to say what they think. As the Communication Style name says, they are willing to challenge the ideas and facts of others. Sometimes this can lead to the perception that they are insensitive.

QUICK SUMMARY AND CROSS-REFERENCE

Primary Motivation	Action
Secondary Motivation	Order
Most Likely to Have Conflict With	Counselor
Also Likely to Have Conflict With	Influencer, Supporter, Advocate
366 Solar Executives Who Are Challengers	Russell Davis

HOW TO BE MOST EFFECTIVE WITH A CHALLENGER

- Get to the point fairly quickly.
- Give them the "big picture" and then be prepared with details if needed.
- Focus on the goal and what it will take to get there.

THE PEOPLE STYLES

The Communication Styles that are primarily motivated by People and relationships are in the upper right section of the *Communication Styles 2.0 Circle of Styles.*

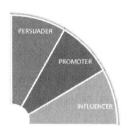

The primary People Style is the Promoter with the Persuader and Influencer also showing a significant amount of People motivation. The Director and Appraiser are blends that feature People as their primary motivation.

SHARED CHARACTERISTICS OF THE PEOPLE STYLES

- These are open Communication Styles that are passionate, engaging, and enthusiastic
- These Styles enjoy people and like to have fun
- Expect them to tell a lot of stories, especially about people
- They see every interaction as an opportunity to build new relationships or strengthen existing ones
- They are not afraid to express emotions and rarely feel self-conscious
- They can easily inspire and charm others
- They tend to focus on the positive and may not understand why people are negative

THE PERSUADER

The primary interest of a Persuader when communicating is getting people to adopt their ideas.

Persuaders are great natural communicators. They can be charming and clear so people want to listen to them and understand what they have to say. They have a natural ability to get people to adopt their ideas and buy their products and can usually make a good argument for almost anything.

QUICK SUMMARY AND CROSS-REFERENCE

Primary Motivation	People
Secondary Motivation	Action
Most Likely to Have Conflict With	Perfectionist
Also Likely to Have Conflict With	Analyzer, Investigator, Contemplator
366 Solar Executives Who Are Persuaders	Grayson Orr

HOW TO BE MOST EFFECTIVE WITH A PERSUADER

- Invest time in building a relationship as it is important and will help you to get things done.
- You will get the best results when you give them a specific goal to focus on and gently follow up to make sure they are on track.
- Be enthusiastic, talk about options, and be willing to listen.

THE PROMOTER

The primary interests of a Promoter when communicating are people and fun.

Promoters have strong social skills and this makes it easy for them to talk to almost anyone. They are very good at winning over people, crowds, even their enemies. They usually have lots of friends and enjoy being in the limelight.

QUICK SUMMARY AND CROSS-REFERENCE

Primary Motivation	People
Secondary Motivation	
Most Likely to Have Conflict With	Analyzer
Also Likely to Have Conflict With	Solver, Perfectionist, Contemplator
366 Solar Executives Who Are Promoters	Barbara Cole

HOW TO BE MOST EFFECTIVE WITH A PROMOTER

- For a Promoter the relationship is part of the task so allow for plenty of talk and social time.
- Be sure to provide lots of recognition and praise when it is appropriate.
- Talk more about what is right rather than what is wrong.

THE INFLUENCER

The primary interest of an Influencer when communicating is building and maintaining relationships.

Influencers communicate easily and get along effortlessly with most people. It is easy for them to express their ideas in terms that others can understand and they are naturally persuasive without being pushy.

QUICK SUMMARY AND CROSS-REFERENCE

Primary Motivation	People
Secondary Motivation	Safety
Most Likely to Have Conflict With	Solver
Also Likely to Have Conflict With	Challenger, Analyzer, Contemplator
366 Solar Executives Who Are Influencers	

HOW TO BE MOST EFFECTIVE WITH AN INFLUENCER

- Be enthusiastic, talk about options, and be willing to listen.
- Ask for their input into decisions.
- Focus more on how your plans will benefit people rather than on the vision behind the plan.

THE SAFETY STYLES

The Communication Styles that are primarily motivated by Safety are located in the lower right section of the *Communication Styles 2.0 Circle of Styles*.

The primary Safety Style is the Supporter with the Counselor and Investigator also showing a significant amount of Safety motivation. The Advocate and Achiever are blends that include Safety as their primary motivation.

SHARED CHARACTERISTICS OF THE SAFETY STYLES

- They are easy to get along with and communicate more by listening than talking
- Soft-spoken and generally good listeners.
- They might be reluctant to give an opinion without encouragement
- They place a high value on avoiding conflict and mistakes so they might not speak up if they disagree
- They tend to trust everyone even if they don't deserve it
- Safety Styles prefer group communication rather than one-on-one

THE COUNSELOR

The primary interest for a Counselor Style when communicating is building and maintaining relationships while minimizing mistakes and problems.

Counselors are seen as positive, warm, and affirming and they have a natural talent for building morale among co-workers.

QUICK SUMMARY AND CROSS-REFERENCE

Primary Motivation	Safety
Secondary Motivation	People
Most Likely to Have Conflict With	Challenger
Also Likely to Have Conflict With	Doer, Solver, Contemplator, Chancellor
366 Solar Executives Who Are Counselors	

HOW TO BE MOST EFFECTIVE WITH A COUNSELOR

- Allow time for small talk and make sure everyone is heard.
- Be friendly, seek compromise, allow time to digest potential change.
- Let them know in a friendly way exactly what is expected and make sure they <u>understand</u> your expectations.

THE SUPPORTER

The primary interests of a Supporter when communicating are relationships and avoiding conflict.

Supporters are excellent friends and confidants. They are peace makers who seek to minimize conflict.

QUICK SUMMARY AND CROSS-REFERENCE

Primary Motivation	Safety
Secondary Motivation	
Most Likely to Have Conflict With	Doer
Also Likely to Have Conflict With	Challenger, Motivator, Chancellor
366 Solar Executives Who Are Supporters	Emily Reed

HOW TO BE MOST EFFECTIVE WITH A SUPPORTER

- Be friendly and explain how what you are saying will benefit the people involved.
- Earn their trust in small steps and don't go for big decisions quickly.
- Take time to build a relationship and consider how what you say will impact your relationship.

THE INVESTIGATOR

The primary interest of an Investigator when communicating is finding answers.

They will be more focused on details rather than the big picture. The Investigator will seek to find answers and solve problems. This is both their strength and weakness.

QUICK SUMMARY AND CROSS-REFERENCE

Primary Motivation	Safety
Secondary Motivation	Order
Most Likely to Have Conflict With	Motivator
Also Likely to Have Conflict With	Doer, Persuader, Chancellor
366 Solar Executives Who Are Investigators	Trisha Mitchell

HOW TO BE MOST EFFECTIVE WITH AN INVESTIGATOR

- Communicate as logically as you can and ask questions to check their understanding.
- Be positive and optimistic in your communications and provide assurance that things will turn out well.
- Details are important to an Investigator so be sure to provide as many details as they need and answer all of their questions.

THE ORDER STYLES

The Communication Styles that are primarily motivated by Order are found in the lower left section of the *Communication Styles 2.0 Circle of Styles*.

The primary Communication Style that is motivated by Order is the Analyzer with the Solver and Perfectionist also showing a significant amount of Order motivation. In addition, the Contemplator and Practitioner are blends that have Order as their primary motivation.

SHARED CHARACTERISTICS OF THE ORDER STYLES

- Typically calm, collected, and matter of fact
- Naturally introverted and feel more comfortable in small groups
- Precise, factual, and direct communication without stories or embellishment
- These Styles are data oriented and organized and expect you to be also
- Can be a perfectionist with what some might think are impossibly high standards
- Prefer to communicate using lists, charts, graphs, and reports

THE PERFECTIONIST

As their Style name suggests, the primary interest of a Perfectionist when communicating is making sure that things are right.

The Perfectionist is the type of person who uses a methodical problem solving approach to life. They tend to lean more toward good ideas, complex concepts, and intriguing solutions rather than toward feelings.

QUICK SUMMARY AND CROSS-REFERENCE

Primary Motivation	Order
Secondary Motivation	Safety
Most Likely to Have Conflict With	Persuader
Also Likely to Have Conflict With	Motivator, Promoter, Director
366 Solar Executives Who Are Perfectionists	

HOW TO BE MOST EFFECTIVE WITH A PERFECTIONIST

- Be sure to provide lots of details up front without them having to ask.
- Be prepared to answer their questions as they will probably bring up points that you have not previously thought about.
- Make changes slowly and make sure they understand the logic behind the change.

THE ANALYZER

The primary interests of the Analyzer when communicating are facts and data.

The Analyzer uses a logical, methodical problem solving approach to life and communication. They will tend to get to the point and explain things logically and back up their logic with data and facts.

QUICK SUMMARY AND CROSS-REFERENCE

Primary Motivation	Order
Secondary Motivation	
Most Likely to Have Conflict With	Promoter
Also Likely to Have Conflict With	Persuader, Influencer, Director
366 Solar Executives Who Are Analyzers	Tyler Hughes

HOW TO BE MOST EFFECTIVE WITH AN ANALYZER

- The Analyzer is a detail-oriented person and quality is important to them so make sure that you have checked your work before giving it to them.
- Get to the point fairly quickly.
- Be prepared to answer questions and prove your point using logic rather than emotion.

THE SOLVER

The main interest of a Solver when communicating is to make sure that plans are made and solutions are implemented.

Their Communication Style can be direct and sometimes confrontational. They are not afraid to ask the tough questions needed to solve problems and will speak up when necessary.

QUICK SUMMARY AND CROSS-REFERENCE

Primary Motivation	Order
Secondary Motivation	Action
Most Likely to Have Conflict With	Influencer
Also Likely to Have Conflict With	Promoter, Counselor, Director
366 Solar Executives Who Are Solvers	Stacy O'Sullivan

HOW TO BE MOST EFFECTIVE WITH A SOLVER

- Remind them of the big picture and team vision when necessary.
- Take a logical approach and let them come to the conclusion on their own without telling them what they should do or think.
- Don't engage in an argument directly, rather ask them questions that make your point.

366 Solar

One of the best ways for you to lock in your understanding of Communication Styles is to "see" them in action.

Of course, since this is a book there's no video but in this section, we're going to meet the people who work at 366 Solar, a solar energy company with an innovative new solar panel fighting for market share.

Along the way, you'll meet the different Communication Styles and be able to observe them in action. You'll see where they get along easily and where their differing Styles cause problems.

Just like any other group of people, they'll have their struggles and victories and you can read about them as the story unfolds.

After each story, there will be an opportunity for you to diagnose the communication problem and offer suggestions. Then we'll replay the story to see how the characters adjust to each other to get the results they need to move the project and company forward.

So that you can get the most out of this section, the stories have been group by the motivations of the characters. This will give you a logical progression you can follow and learn from.

Enjoy!

ACTION STYLES

A DOER (ACTION) WITH A SUPPORTER (SAFETY)

Of course there are almost endless possible combinations of styles working together, and in this story we'll meet Paul Morgan the CEO of 366 Solar and Emily Reed who is the Chief Experience Officer.

Since their styles are opposite each other on Circle of Styles, there's a natural conflict between them when they communicate.

Let's meet them now.

MEET THE PEOPLE

Name	Role	Communication Style	Motivation
Paul Morgan	CEO	Doer	Action
Emily Reed	Chief Experience Officer	Supporter	Safety

MONDAY

Paul Morgan, the CEO of 366 Solar, stalked the hallways of his company.

He had led it from a feisty startup with an innovative product to an organization on the verge of something big, a bid to build a solar array for the University of Alta California. They had a meeting at the end of this week to review their budget and decide if they would move forward.

We've come a long way, he thought. What had started in his garage as a breakthrough in solar panel technology had gone through several rounds of financing and turned into a company with over 150 employees fighting for market share.

He had even managed to win a federal grant that propelled them even further on the journey to providing renewable and sustainable energy.

And on that journey he had assembled a diverse crew to man his ship. Each one of them had their own style, their own way of communicating. Because of that, they didn't always see eye to eye, but it was part of what made the company such a special place. *Most of the time,* he thought with a smile.

He was on his way to see one of them right now. Emily Reed was the most recent addition to the company team. As they had grown into a recognizable brand, he had found the need to hire a Chief Experience Officer. He needed help to enhance his brand's user experience in order to gain market share. Emily was a bit quiet for Paul's taste but he tended to overshadow everybody anyway. And everybody had usually followed his lead and respected his decisions.

Up until now.

Paul stopped outside Emily's office. He traced his fingers over the lettering of the tinted window: Customer Experience Officer. He was about to knock on the glass when he overheard the mumble of a conversation. *Who is she talking to?* he thought to himself as he paced back and forth. *I've got a meeting with Russell Davis today and I always need to be on my toes around him. That old man just loves wasting my time.*

On the other side of the door, Emily was on the phone with Barbara Cole, the company's Marketing Director. *This is just terrible timing. Doesn't he realize how this could affect our customer's experience. This makes my job harder than it needs to be.*

"I just heard about it myself," she said into the phone. "Well, you know Paul better than I do." Becoming a part of 366 Solar had been a dream come true. She had been captivated by Paul's drive and wanted to support that vision. So far, she had managed to add some structure to a company that had been basically moving along on Paul's energy. She had found that she would need to help him understand how his technology provided more than just energy to their customers. And with their different ways of communicating, Emily knew it would be hard.

From outside, Paul sensed a lull in her conversation. *This can't wait,* he thought and knocked on the door. Emily was at a loss as to who to respond to. For Paul, the reply was too long in coming and he opened the door. He walked inside as she turned to face him. *Well, speak of the devil,* she thought.

Emily raised her hand, trying to let Paul know she was going to end the call. She knew how impatient he could be. She spoke into the phone. "I've got to let you go. I'll call you back." Emily hit end on her cell phone and put it down. She stood up to greet Paul.

"Hey Paul. How're you? I heard your wife had surgery. How's she feeling?"

What? he thought to himself. *How is that relevant right now?* Paul shrugged off her question. "You wanted to talk about the prototype. What's up?"

Emily found herself taken aback for a second. She hadn't yet gotten used to his brusque manner. *This is not going to be easy,* she thought. "We shouldn't do that yet."

"Shouldn't?" Paul asked. "What do you mean shouldn't?"

"That's not where we're supposed to be yet. I really think we should run some more tests before ordering a production on the prototype." *He's jumping the gun. I've got to get him to see that.* Emily knew that Tyler Hughes, the CFO for 366 Solar, was still on the fence about the bid. It was a bold move but one fraught with risk. *We haven't even reviewed our budget.*

"Tests are a waste of time. I want something to show the people of Alta California."

"But we haven't even made a decision on that Paul," she said, a nervous tone creeping into her voice. "That's why we're meeting on Friday. Why are you rushing forward to—

"The panels work. You know that. The engineers know that."

"Listen, I—"

Paul raised his hands in the air in frustration. *Why doesn't she get it?* Paul asked himself. *She's obsessed over needless details.* "It's ready. We're moving ahead."

Emily stared at him in silence. "Are you sure about this?"

"Of course I'm sure! I don't want to waste any more time than we absolutely have to. We need that contract. You understand that, right?"

Emily cast her eyes down. "I do."

"Don't worry. I got us this far."

"Yes, you did," Emily said.

Paul smiled. "Great." He turned abruptly and left the office. Emily sighed with relief, but there was still worry in her mind. *I still think we should wait. He doesn't seem to value what I bring to the table, Maybe I was wrong about joining the company.*

Meanwhile, Paul picked up his pace down the hallway. *Problem solved,* he thought. *On to the next one.*

HERE'S WHAT'S HAPPENING

As you can see, this level of conflict is most likely to occur when the styles are directly across from each other on the *Circle*. Let's look at the possible sources of conflict between the two styles:

Action Styles like to push the envelope while Safety Styles tend to prefer the traditional way of doing things. A Safety Style will be inclined to follow existing policies and rules while an Action Style may seek to challenge them. Action Styles can be so focused on achieving results that they may overlook small details. Safety Styles tend to plan and strategize every aspect of a project.

An Action Style is more vested in the communication process when it's more evident that it aligns with his tasks and objectives.

THINK ABOUT THIS

How could Emily Reed have communicated in a way that would align the conversation with Paul Morgan's objectives?

How could Paul have reacted better to Emily's concerns?

Action and Safety Styles are bound to have differences, but when they understand each other these two Communication Styles can form an excellent team.

The following replay shows how the two types *could* respond to each other if they were more self-aware of their motivations and the Circle of Styles.

LET'S TRY THAT AGAIN

Paul Morgan, the CEO of 366 Solar, stalked the hallways of his company.

He had led it from a feisty startup with an innovative product to an organization on the verge of something big, a bid to build a solar array for the University of Alta California. They had a meeting at the end of this week to review their budget and decide if they would move forward.

We've come a long way, he thought. What had started in his garage as a breakthrough in solar panel technology had gone through several rounds of financing and turned into a company with over 150 employees fighting for market share. He had even managed to win a federal grant that propelled them even further on the journey to providing renewable and sustainable energy.

And on that journey he had assembled a diverse crew to man his ship. Each one of them had their own style, their own way of communicating. Because of that, they didn't always see eye to eye, but it was part of what made the company such a special place. *Most of the time,* he thought with a smile.

He was on his way to see one of them right now. Emily Reed was the most recent addition to the company team. As they had grown into a recognizable brand, he had found the need to hire a Chief Experience Officer. He needed help to enhance his brand's user experience in order to gain market share. Emily was a bit quiet for Paul's taste but he tended to overshadow everybody anyway. And everybody had usually followed his lead and respected his decisions.

Up until now.

Paul stopped outside Emily's office. He traced his fingers over the lettering of the tinted window: Customer Experience Officer. He was about to knock on the glass when he overheard the mumble of a conversation. *Who is she talking to?* he thought to himself as he paced back and forth. *I've got a meeting with Russell Davis today and I always need to be on my toes around him. That old man just loves wasting my time.*

On the other side of the door, Emily was on the phone with Barbara Cole, the company's Marketing Director. *This is just terrible timing. Doesn't he realize how this could affect our customer's experience. This makes my job harder than it needs to be.*

"I just heard about it myself," she said into the phone. "Well, you know Paul better than I do." Becoming a part of 366 Solar had been a dream come true. She had been captivated by Paul's drive and wanted to support that vision. So far, she had managed to add some structure to a company that had been basically moving along on Paul's energy. She had found that she would need to help him understand how his technology provided more than just energy to their customers. And with their different ways of communicating, Emily knew it would be hard.

From outside, Paul sensed a lull in her conversation. *This can't wait,* he thought and knocked on the door. Emily was at a loss as to who to respond to. For Paul, the reply was too long in coming and he opened the door. He walked inside as she turned to face him. *Well, speak of the devil,* she thought.

Emily raised her hand, trying to let Paul know she was going to end the call. She knew how impatient he could be. She spoke into the phone. "I've got to let you go. I'll call you back." Emily hit end on her cell phone and put it down. She stood up to greet Paul.

"Hey Paul. How're you? I heard your wife had surgery. How's she feeling?"

What? he thought to himself. *How is that relevant right now?* Paul shrugged off her question. "You wanted to talk about the prototype. What's up?"

Emily found herself taken aback for a second. She hadn't yet gotten used to his brusque manner. *This is not going to be easy,* she thought. "We shouldn't do that yet."

"Shouldn't?" Paul asked. "What do you mean shouldn't?"

"That's not where we're supposed to be yet. I really think we should run some more tests before ordering a production on the prototype." *He's jumping the gun. I've got to get him to see that.* Emily knew that Tyler Hughes, the CFO for 366 Solar, was still on the fence about the bid. It was a bold move but one fraught with risk. *We haven't even reviewed our budget.*

"Tests are a waste of time. I want something to show the people of Alta California."

"But we haven't even made a decision on that Paul," she said, a nervous tone creeping into her voice. "That's why we're meeting on Friday. Why are you rushing forward to—

"The panels work. You know that. The engineers know that."

Emily realized that she had to get Paul to understand her point of view. "I really think we should wait."

"What's the point of waiting?"

Emily took a deep breath. *How do I explain that his drive to move forward might backfire?* "If something goes wrong, what will that say about our product?"

"We won't have a product if we don't gain market share!" Paul paced back and forth in frustration. *Why doesn't she get it? She's so obsessed over details and safety.*

"I need you to see the big picture here. This bid for Alta California will not only give us market share but put us on the map in a big way."

The big picture is all he sees. What he doesn't realize is that big pictures are made up of small brushstrokes. "Listen," Emily said.

"Not everything is about gaining market share. A great company is also defined by great customer experience. A reputation for a great product will last forever."

Her argument hit Paul like a bucket of ice water. "Say that again."

"Which part?"

"The part about lasting forever."

I think I got through to him, she thought. "I know how important sales are to you. And to this company. But as long as we're the best, I think we'll do just fine."

"The best, huh?" Paul replied. "I like the sound of that."

Emily smiled. "I thought you would."

I was so obsessed with getting myself understood that I missed what her real concern was. "What do you propose then?"

"You hired me to go beyond just a product. I want to create a whole user experience around the array for the university. I have something planned and I want to pitch it at the meeting on Friday."

I may have judged her too harshly, Paul thought. *She may be quiet, but she runs deep. It reminds me why I hired her in the first place.* He flashed her a smile.

"Problem solved," Paul said.

Emily laughed. "I think that opportunity taken would be more appropriate."

"I agree," Paul said.

BRINGING OUT THE BEST IN EVERYONE

Action Styles and Safety Styles can work best together when both of them are more aware of their natural tendencies and take them into account during their interactions.

In this replay of events, Paul Morgan was more open to what Emily brought to the table and her need to be safe. Her tendency to avoid conflict and consider the feelings of others serves her well in her customer experience role, but not as well when she knows that she needs to stand up to Paul.

To Emily's credit, she realized what had happened and found a way to help Paul see how her concerns would help him to get what he wanted (a long term viable company) rather than just slow things.

It rarely works well to directly challenge one of the Action Styles because they are likely to push you out of the way or run over you in their desire for action. They might even become a Bully like you'll meet in the section about difficult people.

Here are some tips about how to be more effective when communicating with an Action Style:

- Get to the point fairly quickly.
- Give them the "big picture" and then be prepared with details if requested.
- If you present a problem, come prepared with a solution.
- Answer the question "What are the benefits?" not "How will we get it done?" This is the secret to how Emily won Paul over to her way of thinking.

WHEN AN ACTION STYLE MEETS AN ACTION STYLE

You might think that the Action styles would get along with each other easily because they are the same style. This is true with all of the other motivations, but the Actions not only want to get things done, they tend to want to get them done their way.

Let's listen in on a meeting between Paul Morgan and Russell Davis, an angel investor who is a Challenger and also motivated by action like Paul.

We'll also have Danielle Edmonds present, Paul's executive assistant who is a Blend Style of communicator. As you join the meeting, try to identify the causes of conflict between Paul and Russell and think of what each person could do differently to have a better outcome to the meeting.

Also, pay particular attention to how Danielle, a Blend Style, sees the situation.

MEET THE PEOPLE

Name	Role	Communication Style	Motivation
Paul Morgan	CEO	Doer	Action
Russell Davis	Angel Investor	Challenger	Action
Danielle Edmonds	Executive Assistant	Blend	

MONDAY

As Paul headed back to his office, he spotted Danielle Edmonds, his executive assistant walking toward him.

She had been the first person he hired after he had incorporated and it had been the best decision he'd made.

Her way of communicating always managed to keep him on task and it had defused many conflicts over the years. Paul didn't know what he would do without her. She was the glue that kept everybody together at 366 Solar.

He was about to say 'hi' when he recognized the look on her face.

Paul stopped in his tracks. "He's already here, isn't he?"

Danielle nodded. "Yep. And no, I had no warning. As usual." *Sparks are going to fly,* she thought to herself.

"Great," Paul replied as he moved forward.

Danielle moved into step behind him. Paul rounded the corner and saw the white hair of Russell Davis, the angel investor who had funded Paul's vision for the company. Something that had come at a high cost. *I sometimes wonder if I made the right decision.*

"Hello Russell," Paul said as he walked into his office. From the corner of his eye he saw Danielle give him an encouraging smile. He closed the door and held out his hand.

Russell Davis was a busy man. In his late sixties, he was constantly on the lookout for opportunity. He had found it in Paul Morgan a couple of years ago. Now he was here to make sure that opportunity stayed alive.

But he had become impatient, feeling he had been waiting too long for Paul to show up. And it had done nothing for his mood. "Paul," he said curtly as he shook the offered hand.

"Well, let's get to it," Paul said. He sat down in his chair and looked intently at Russell.

Straight to the point, Russell thought. *I do like that about him.*" Production of the solar panels needs to be moved to China."

"We're not outsourcing."

"Are you aware of what's happening in the news? Utility companies are killing solar with hidden costs."

Why is he bringing this up? It's nothing. "Of course I'm aware. And it doesn't matter. We'll prevail in the end."

Russell shook his head. *He's looking at this the wrong way.* "In the meantime, though, it would be nice to make a profit, don't you think?"

"Production is going to be here. In the States."

"We can make them cheaper in China. I already have the facility. I've talked to the rest of the investors and they're—"

"You did what?!" Pal exclaimed as he stood up. The idea that Russell had taken such a step without him incensed Paul. *How dare he?* He could feel the heat of anger rising on his face.

"Paul, do you have any idea how much money we can save the company by moving production overseas?"

"I don't think you have any idea about what this company stands for, Russell."

Russell shot up from his seat. "I don't?" He took a step toward Paul. "I backed you when no else would. When everybody thought your patent would never come through. Remember that? Remember when you came to me?"

Paul took another step closer. They stood inches from each other. "Yes. And I regret it every day."

No one had ever said anything like that to Russell before. "Paul, I don't think you're fit to head this company anymore."

"I *am* this company!"

Russell buttoned up his suit. "You're not prioritizing the interests of the shareholders."

"I took it from my garage to where we are now!"

Russell turned toward the door. "I'm taking over," he said.

"I'd like to see you try."

"I'll do more than try. You know I own enough stock." Without another word, Russell strode out of the office.

As Russell walked away, Paul slammed the door.

Danielle shook her head. *This was bound to happen someday,* she thought. *For all his drive and vision, Paul was obstinate. And Russell was the exact same way. Putting those two in a room together could be like pouring gasoline on a fire. What are we going to do now?*

HERE'S WHAT'S HAPPENING

As you could see from the story, the majority of conflicts between these styles arise because they are so similar.

Since they are so focused on their own goals, they may ignore the thoughts and feeling of others. Their direct style of communication can sometimes cut other people off. Action Styles can see the other as being less capable.

Since their communication is blunt and straight forward, it leaves little time for interpretation. Action styles don't try to avoid conflict, so when it arises they may find themselves moving forward instead of taking a step back.

THINK ABOUT THIS

How did that play out between Paul and Russell?

Could they have managed their conflict in a different manner?

LET'S TRY THAT AGAIN

As Paul headed back to his office, he spotted Danielle Edmonds, his executive assistant walking toward him.

She had been the first person he hired after he had incorporated and it had been the best decision he'd made. Her way of communicating always managed to keep him on task and it had defused many conflicts over the years. Paul didn't know what he would do without her. She was the glue that kept everybody together at 366 Solar.

He was about to say 'hi' when he recognized the look on her face.

Paul stopped in his tracks. "He's already here, isn't he?"

Danielle nodded. "Yep. And no, I had no warning. As usual." *Sparks are going to fly,* she thought to herself.

"Great," Paul replied as he moved forward.

Danielle moved into step behind him. Paul rounded the corner and saw the white hair of Russell Davis, the angel investor who had funded Paul's vision for the company. Something that had come at a high cost. *I sometimes wonder if I made the right decision.*

"Hello Russell," Paul said as he walked into his office. From the corner of his eye he saw Danielle give him an encouraging smile. He closed the door and held out his hand.

Russell Davis was a busy man. In his late sixties, he was constantly on the lookout for opportunity. He had found it in Paul Morgan a couple of years ago. Now he was here to make sure that opportunity stayed alive.

But he had become impatient, feeling he had been waiting too long for Paul to show up. And it had done nothing for his mood. "Paul," he said curtly as he shook the offered hand.

"Well, let's get to it," Paul said. He sat down in his chair and looked intently at Russell.

Straight to the point, Russell thought. *I do like that about him.* " Production of the solar panels needs to be moved to China."

"We're not outsourcing."

"Are you aware of what's happening in the news? Utility companies are killing solar with hidden costs."

Why is he bringing this up? It's nothing. " Of course I'm aware. And it doesn't matter. We'll prevail in the end."

Russell shook his head. *He's looking at this the wrong way.* "In the meantime, though, it would be nice to make a profit, don't you think?"

How can I get him to understand? "I see your point Russell. But here's mine. I want the panels to be made in the States because I want to provide jobs for people here. We're building for our future. To be energy independent. How can we stay true to that vision if we shortchange it for the bottom line?"

That's admirable, Russell thought. *Maybe even poetic.* "But we can't provide any jobs unless this company is successful, Paul."

"Well, think of the quality of our product. Do you speak Chinese?"

Russell laughed. "No."

"Our reputation is just as important as our product. And we can't keep an eye on production as well as we can here. Besides, I don't think either one of us fancies sitting on a plane for that long."

Russell shook his head. "I'm too old for that."

Paul paced the office. "There's a reason you backed me. Do you still believe in that?"

"I do."

"I know that costs are important to you. Let's put our heads together on this. We can find a solution that benefits both of us."

Russell contemplated what Paul was saying. "Mmm. Flights to China are too long, but the flight to Reno isn't."

"What are you talking about?"

"Nevada tax incentive. There's a new governor. If we start up our production facility there, the tax incentive could offset the costs of keeping production stateside."

Paul nodded. "I can put together a proposal. Barbara Cole, our Marketing Director, can work wonders with publicity."

"I can get the ball rolling with the legislature and early committees." *This could be prove to be even better than China,* Russell thought.

Paul stood up and Russell followed suit.

"I remember when I met you," Russell said. "You were working out of your garage. I'm glad to see you've made it this far."

Paul shook his head. "*We've* made it this far. And we'll go even farther."

They shook hands.

"I'll keep you posted." Russell turned and left the office.

Danielle, who had been waiting for the sparks to fly, breathed a sigh of relief. *Well, I'm really glad that worked out.* She had been tempted to intervene but knew it might prove disastrous.

Both of their futures were so tied to the future of the company that they needed to learn to communicate better. So far, it looked like they'd managed to do it.

BRINGING OUT THE BEST IN EVERYONE

When Action Styles can find a common goal, they will be motivated to work together. In this version of events, Paul was able to communicate his goals and objectives to Russell.

Through communication and understanding, they were able to work together to create a new plan that aligned with both of their objectives. They managed to set clear boundaries so that neither of them will step on each other's toes. This keeps the independent nature of the Action Styles content.

WHEN A PEOPLE STYLE MEETS AN ORDER STYLE

Once again, we have two styles that are across from each other on the Circle of Styles so there is a good possibility of conflict.

It's now Tuesday. Let's see what happens when a people style meets an order style.

MEET THE PEOPLE

Name	Role	Communication Style	Motivation
Barbara Cole	Marketing Director	Promoter	People
Tyler Hughes	Chief Financial Officer	Analyzer	Order

TUESDAY

Barbara Cole, the Marketing Director for 366 Solar, strolled past the cafeteria. She spotted Tyler Hughes, the Chief Financial Officer, sitting by himself. *Eating lunch on your own is terrible,* she thought. *I'll go join him.* She switched directions and headed back toward him.

What she didn't know was that Tyler had already seen her pass by. And her coming toward him was the last thing he wanted right now. Barbara was too bubbly for his tastes. Conversations with her always left him exhausted. *I just want to eat my lunch in peace.*

"Hey, Tyler! We missed you at the company meetup this weekend. Even Paul was there! What happened?"

"I couldn't go."

"Oh, is everything alright?"

"Yes. Why wouldn't it be?"

Barbara was struck by his response. *Why is he always so distant? Maybe I just need to get to know him better.* She pulled up a chair and sat next to him.

However, this move intruded on his personal bubble. *Space. I need space!* he thought.

"I just adopted a new dog. Did I tell you? Her name is Bailee. So cute. Want to see some pictures?" Barbara took out her phone and scrolled to find pictures of her dog. She showed them to Tyler. "Look at that face!"

The phone was too close for him to look properly. *I need to get this over with.* "Yes. Beautiful."

"Do you have any pets?"

"Look, I've got to go. Numbers to crunch."

"Numbers! You're such an expert, Tyler. You're an incredible addition to the team."

Always with the compliments, he thought. *She rambles on so much I wonder how she has time to do her own job.* "Thanks."

"Actually, now that you mentioned it, well, I mean I mentioned it, I wanted to talk to you about something. The marketing budget is underfunded. We need to allocate more funds for social media."

"What for?"

What for? What does he mean what for? "Well, you know Paul is set to bid on the contract for Alta California. I think we should increase our awareness among millennials. They are the future, after all, and will help propel us forward into gaining market share once they graduate."

Tyler started to worry. "I haven't gotten any emails about this."

"I want to do a campaign directed toward them. I'm thinking a push on social media, and, wait, I got it! We'll do a video, release it on YouTube, push it to go viral."

Whose decision was this? Tyler thought. *And why wasn't I told about it?*

Barbara was on a roll. This was where she felt the most comfortable, letting the ideas flow, bouncing them off others. "You know what? We could focus on the company! On us. A small documentary. Intimate. Right? Just picture it." Barbara took her phone out and started recording Tyler. "The camera on you while they ask about your experiences in the company. Your hopes. I know just the people for it, too."

The mere thought of that intimidated Tyler. *I don't want anybody filming me.* He had to get her to calm down. "Barbara, stop."

Barbara flinched as if he had struck her. "Stop?"

"You're just saying the first things that come to your mind."

Whoa, Barbara thought. *He's not distant. He's just mean.* "Come on, Tyler. I need you to keep up with me here."

Tyler stared at her. He gathered what remained of his lunch and stood up. "Why don't we shelve it for now and bring it back up when you've got a better handle on it." He walked to the trash container and dumped his tray. *I need some down time.* Without a glance backward he left for his office.

Well, Barbara thought. *That certainly didn't go well.*

HERE'S WHAT'S HAPPENING

Conflict tends to arise when one Communication Style expects the other to share his or her strengths. To avoid conflict and work best together, it is important that both parties understand these differences. Let's look at the possible sources of conflict between the two styles:

- Order Styles tend to be analytical thinkers who thrive on solving problems.
- Freedom and privacy are important to Order Styles. They like people, but too much social interaction can leave them feeling drained and exhausted.

THINK ABOUT THIS

How could Barbara have approached Tyler differently?

What should Tyler have said to understand Barbara's goal?

Their differences in Communication Styles can complement each other. Understanding these differences is the key to a successful working relationship. If both parties focus on what they do best, projects can be completed successfully.

LET'S TRY THAT AGAIN

Here's how the two types *could* respond to each other if they were more self-aware of their communication styles.

Barbara Cole, the Marketing Director for 366 Solar, strolled past the cafeteria. She spotted Tyler Hughes, the Chief Financial Officer, sitting by himself. *I wonder if he's alright with eating lunch on his own?* she thought. *He always seems to do it.* She stopped in her tracks and headed over to him.

What she didn't know was that Tyler had already seen her pass by. And her coming toward him was the last thing he wanted right now. Barbara was too bubbly for his tastes.

Conversations with her always left him exhausted. *I just want to eat my lunch in peace.*

"Hey, Tyler! Is it alright if I join you for a bit?"

"I think so," he replied, surprised at her request to join him. Barbara was the type to go up to anybody and talk to them.

"We missed you at the company meetup this weekend. Even Paul was there! What happened?"

"I couldn't go."

"Oh, is everything alright?"

"Yes. Why wouldn't it be?"

Barbara was struck by his response. *Why is he always so distant? Or maybe he just likes his space?* Realizing that, Barbara scooted backward a bit. *There we go.* "I only asked because we'd like to see more of you. But I get that we all need some down time."

"Even you?" Tyler asked.

Barbara laughed. "Yeah, even me. Listen, I realize this may not be the best time and place, but I wanted to mention the funds allocated to social media."

"What about them? They're what was approved last meeting."

"I realize that but I've had some ideas. I want increase our awareness among millennials. They are the future, after all, and will help propel us forward into gaining market share once they graduate. "

That's not a bad idea, Tyler thought. "I can see how that's important. But I haven't gotten any emails about it."

"Oh, no, it's not at that stage yet. Just wanted to bounce some ideas off of you. Nothing definitive."

"I can try."

"I'm thinking a push on social media, and, wait, I got it! We'll do a video, release it on YouTube, push it to go viral." Barbara felt the floodgates start to loosen. She looked over at Tyler and saw the discomfort on his face. *I may be going too fast for him.* "Look, how about I come up with something more concrete and bring it to you."

"I can definitely help you with that," Tyler replied. "We can look at budgets, set up a timeline for release, analyze possible conversion rates."

"That's a great idea! I know that's not my strong point." *I've heard people say Tyler can be cold, but I think they just don't know how to talk to him.* "I appreciate it."

"Of course."

"I'll leave you to your lunch. I'll send you an email once I have things written down. Maybe by Thursday? First thing? We can meet at my office."

"Sounds good." *That wasn't so painful,* Tyler thought. He made a mental note to set aside Thursday morning for her. It could prove useful to have that information at the meeting Friday.

Barbara walked away with a new bounce in her step. *I've got to pitch this to Grayson,* she thought. Grayson Orr, their Public Relations Officer, could definitely help whip this into something she could take to Emily and Paul.

BRINGING OUT THE BEST IN EVERYONE

People Styles and Order Styles can work together when they are self-aware of how they communicate.

People Styles tend to struggle in areas relating to analysis, organization, and planning, which is an area of strength for Order Styles.

The Analyzer wants to gather as many facts, and as much information, as they can before moving ahead. As you could see from these interactions, this is not something at which Barbara excels.

In this version of events, Barbara was able to identify Tyler's need for space. In return, Tyler recognized the innovation that she brought to the table and offered his own skills in tempering that into something that would benefit both themselves and the company.

WHEN A PEOPLE STYLE MEETS A PEOPLE STYLE

The attributes of the People Communication Styles tend to leave little room for conflict. Since they focus on the positive aspects of a situation and enjoy interacting with others, they are inclined to get along with members in all levels of an organization. When conflict does to arise, they can usually sort it out due to their people-focused Communication Styles.

On the other hand, their enthusiasm for social interaction may sometimes intrude on their responsibilities. Because of this, important problems may be overlooked in favor of future possibilities and ideas. The following story will illustrate some of these tendencies.

MEET THE PEOPLE

Name	Role	Communication Style	Motivation
Barbara Cole	Human Resources	Promoter	People
Grayson Orr	Public Relations	Persuader	People
Danielle Edmonds	Executive Assistant	Blend	

TUESDAY

Danielle could hear the laughter all the way in her office. Her mouth twisted to the side. *Whenever those two got together, it was always a riot,* she thought. *But there's no doubting their talent.*

Barbara Cole's marketing efforts had helped put 366 Solar on the map. And the PR work Grayson did had gotten them on the first page of all of the major search engines and a section in Wikipedia.

Danielle knew they had both received offers from other firms. Thankfully, Paul had stepped in and matched the offers. However, this left Danielle with the sometimes difficult task of reining them in. Danielle sighed, stood up, and began making her way toward Barbara's office. She knocked on the door twice, then once more.

Inside the office, Barbara recognized Danielle's knock immediately. Grayson was not so quick to catch on.

"Come on in!" Grayson said. "The more the merrier!"

Barbara shook her head. "You know this is *my* office right?"

"It's a nice one. Maybe I should move my desk in?"

"Right."

Danielle pushed the door open. "Hey guys. Have you got a couple of minutes?"

Grayson smiled widely. "Always."

He's not as charming as he thinks, Danielle thought. *Still, he's always courteous and usually knows what to say.*

"I'm sorry if we were too loud," Barbara said. "We just got carried away with our media launch."

Danielle raised an eyebrow. "Media launch?" Grayson offered Danielle a chair. She declined. "What media launch?"

"Nothing definitive yet," Grayson said.

"Because we still need—

"But think of this," Grayson interrupted. "The desert. Vast. Empty. But a potential provenance of energy independence."

"I like that." Barbara said.

Grayson nodded. "Did you see what I did there with the alliteration?"

"Oh, I heard it," Barbara replied.

"Great title for a press release. Guaranteed media pickup."

Danielle felt like she was getting left behind. "Whoa. Hold on. What press release?"

"You know," Barbara said.

"No, I don't."

"The factory we're building in Nevada."

How did they hear about that? Danielle wondered. *Never mind, these two know everybody. It's their job.* "I don't think we're ready for that."

Why is she being so negative? Barbara asked herself. "We're just thinking ahead." Grayson nodded in support.

Danielle shook her head. "We need to focus on the present. I looked at the website. It still crashes. And Grayson, we still need a press release on how we've implemented the grant we received." Danielle could feel her words making the duo instantly uncomfortable.

"That's such old news," Grayson replied. "It's not exciting anymore!"

"Well, it still needs to get done."

"Come on. What about a series of short videos instead? Handheld. Documentary style."

Barbara's eyes lit up. "You know what? I had the exact same idea. It would help the public to relate to what we're doing here."

"I know, right?"

"I pitched it to Tyler, but I'm not sure he was feeling it."

Danielle stared as they both ignored her and continued to bounce the idea back and forth. *If I don't stop them now, this will go on all day. But it has to be done right.*

HOW CAN THE PEOPLE STYLES WORK TOGETHER?

The spirited nature of the People Style of communication tends to lead them into new and exciting opportunities. They seek to act immediately on opportunities but they may overlook potential obstacles. What could Danielle have done to rein in the enthusiastic excesses of Grayson and Barbara?

The following alternative scenario shows how the People Styles could respond if they had more knowledge of the Communication Styles.

LET'S TRY THAT AGAIN

Danielle could hear the laughter all the way in her office. Her mouth twisted to the side. *Whenever those two got together, it was always a riot,* she thought. *But there's no doubting their talent.* Barbara Cole's marketing efforts had helped put 366 Solar on the map. And the PR work Grayson did had gotten them on the first page of all of the major search engines and a section in Wikipedia.

Danielle knew they had both received offers from other firms. Thankfully, Paul had stepped in and matched the offers. However, this left Danielle with the sometimes difficult task of reining them in.

Danielle sighed, stood up, and began making her way toward Barbara's office. She knocked on the door twice, then once more.

Inside the office, Barbara recognized Danielle's knock immediately. Grayson was not so quick to catch on.

"Come on in!" Grayson said. "The more the merrier!"

Barbara shook her head. "You know this is *my* office right?"

"It's a nice one. Maybe I should move my desk in?"

"Right."

Danielle pushed the door open. "Hey guys. Have you got a couple of minutes?"

Grayson smiled widely. "Always."

He's not as charming as he thinks, Danielle thought. *Still, he's always courteous and usually knows what to say.*

"I'm sorry if we were too loud," Barbara said. "We just got carried away with our media launch."

Danielle raised an eyebrow. "Media launch?" Grayson offered Danielle a chair. She declined. "What media launch?"

"Nothing definitive yet," Grayson said.

"Because we still need—

"But think of this," Grayson interrupted. "The desert. Vast. Empty. But a potential provenance of energy independence."

"I like that." Barbara said.

Grayson nodded. "Did you see what I did there with the alliteration?

"I heard."

"Great title for a press release. Guaranteed media pickup."

Danielle felt like she was getting left behind. "Whoa. Hold on. What press release?"

"You know," Barbara said.

"No, I don't."

"The factory we're building in Nevada."

How did they hear about that? Danielle wondered. *Never mind, these two know everybody. It's their job to know.* "I don't think we're ready for anybody to know about that."

Why is she being so negative? Barbara thought. "We're just thinking ahead." Grayson nodded in support.

If I don't stop them now, this could go on all day. But it has to be done right. Danielle liked to think of herself as the fire department. She put out blazes when they occurred and stopped others from starting in the first place.

"Thinking of the future is good," Danielle said. "But the present still demands our attention. I can see that you guys have been working hard on this. I appreciate what that could mean for the company."

Oh, wait, she's not mad, Grayson thought.

"I know you like to bounce ideas off of each other, but I'm afraid we might fall behind schedule."

"I understand," Barbara replied. *I see where she's coming from.* "How's this? We'll take care of the present needs of the company first."

Grayson jumped in after Barbara finished. "Then we'll get into future mode."

"Sounds good to me," Danielle replied.

BRINGING OUT THE BEST IN EVERYONE

When People Styles find themselves working together on a project, they may have difficulty staying on task, especially when they don't find the work exciting.

Since they tend to avoid structure and prefer the big picture over details, it's a good idea for them to think of structure and become more grounded.

Not only will they get more work done, but it will reduce conflict with others in the organization.

SAFETY STYLE WITH ACTION STYLE

When Action and Safety Styles come into contact, there is some potential for conflict. Since they lie at opposite sides of the Circle of Styles, their differing styles can cause problems.

However, that does not mean they can't communicate successfully.

MEET THE PEOPLE

Name	Role	Communication Style	Motivation
Emily Reed	Chief Experience Officer	Supporter	Safety
Harold Dunn	Chief Technical Officer	Motivator	Action
Danielle Edmonds	Executive Assistant	Blend	
Tyler Hughes	Chief Financial Officer	Analyzer	Order

WEDNESDAY

Emily was starting to feel the pressure.

The meeting to review the bid for the array was now just two days away. She had been working with Harold Dunn, the Chief Technical Officer for 366 Solar, on enhancing the user experience for their customers. She hoped to be able to add that to their bid. She knew the system was still weeks away from launch, but Harold kept insisting on meeting. She had called in Tyler for some extra insight.

Harold Dunn paced around the conference room. *Why is she so slow?* he thought to himself. His team had been working day and night on the new application for 366 Solar. He had pushed them to get the app ready and they had delivered.

He was proud of his team. He had handpicked them, eschewing the traditional method of going to the top tier universities. Instead, he went for less recognized schools, confident that he could find the talent he needed. He had been right. *There's no time for second guessing,* he thought. That was his personal philosophy and how he operated.

Tyler Hughes walked toward the conference room. He had an inkling of what might go down. Harold could be something of a loose cannon. *A lot like Paul,* he thought to himself. Tyler recognized his good ideas. *But he definitely needs to be restrained sometimes. Especially now that we have that meeting coming up.* He stepped inside the conference room and was greeted by Harold's wide grin.

"Tyler!" Harold said, coming up close to shake his hand. Harold's demeanor was always pleasant. His style of communication allowed him to work the room and get along with everybody. Tyler preferred to keep himself calm and collected, but he would speak up if needed, sometimes even to the detriment of people's feelings.

"I assume Emily is on her way," Tyler said.

"I hope so. I've got good news. The app is ready."

"Let's wait until she gets here."

Just then, Emily walked into the room. "I'm here, gentlemen." She was carrying a box of donuts along with her satchel. She set them down on the table. "I brought something for all of us."

Tyler smiled. Emily was always thinking of others. It was just who she was.

"I'm good, thanks. Emily, the app is ready."

But some people don't seem to see, Tyler thought. *I hope Emily understands that.*

"The app is ready?" Emily had been working with Harold to create an application that would keep track of the energy expenditure of each customer's solar array. Not only that, it also used the mobile phone's camera to measure the intensity of the sunlight to calculate how much power each panel could generate. It could help pull customers away from the competition when they realized how much more they could save by switching to 366 Solar.

"We can launch yesterday," Harold stated.

"We're not going to do that," Emily replied.

Harold huffed. "And why not?"

"We're not ready."

Tyler leaned back in his chair. *I wonder how she's going to get him to understand that?*

HERE'S WHAT'S HAPPENING

When the Communication Styles are directly opposite to each other, there is potential for conflict. They see situations from their own viewpoint and have difficulty understanding what the other is thinking.

The Safety Styles look to minimize risks. To them, Action Styles can appear to be making decisions without appropriately considering the consequences.

The Safety Styles' commitment to detail can cause problems when making big picture decisions. An Action Style is more vested in the communication process when it's more evident that it aligns with his or her tasks and objectives.

THINK ABOUT THIS

How can Emily help Harold to see the risks of launching too soon?

What can Emily do to help his decision making process?

On top of everything else, we have Tyler Hughes, an Order Style, expressing his own concern for the project.

As more of the Styles come into contact with each other, we can see how complex creating a harmonious environment can be. If the Styles fail to take these Style differences into consideration, communication can fall apart.

Some conflict is inevitable between Action and Safety Styles, but with a little effort they can team up with superior results. The following story shows one possible way.

LET'S TRY THAT AGAIN

Emily was starting to feel the pressure. The meeting to review the bid for the array was now just two days away. She had been working with Harold Dunn, the Chief Technical Officer for 366 Solar, on enhancing the user experience for their customers. She hoped to be able to add that to their bid. She knew the system was still weeks away from launch, but Harold kept insisting on meeting. She had called in Tyler for some extra insight.

Harold Dunn paced around the conference room. *Why is she so slow?* he thought to himself. His team had been working day and night on the new application for 366 Solar. He had pushed them to get the app ready and they had delivered. He was proud of his team. He had handpicked them, eschewing the traditional method of going to the top tier universities. Instead, he went for less recognized schools, confident that he could find the talent he needed. He had been right. *There's no time for second guessing,* he thought. That was his personal philosophy and how he operated.

Tyler Hughes walked toward the conference room. He had an inkling of what might go down. Harold could be something of a loose cannon. *A lot like Paul,* he thought to himself. Tyler recognized his good ideas. *But he definitely needs to be restrained sometimes. Especially now that we have that meeting coming up.* He stepped inside the conference room and was greeted by Harold's wide grin.

"Tyler!" Harold said, coming up close to shake his hand. Harold's demeanor was always pleasant. His style of communication allowed him to work the room and get along with everybody. Tyler preferred to keep himself calm and collected, but he would speak up if needed, sometimes even to the detriment of people's feelings.

"I assume Emily is on her way," Tyler said.

"I hope so. I've got good news. The app is ready."

"Let's wait until she gets here."

Just then, Emily walked into the room. "I'm here, gentlemen." She was carrying a box of donuts along with her satchel. She set them down on the table. "I brought something for all of us."

Tyler smiled. Emily was always thinking of others. It was just who she was.

"I'm good, thanks. Emily, the app is ready."

But some people don't seem to see, Tyler thought. *I hope Emily understands that.*

"The app is ready?" Emily had been working with Harold to create an application that would keep track of the energy expenditure of each customer's solar array. Not only that, it also used the mobile phone's camera to measure the intensity of the sunlight to calculate how much power each panel could generate. It could help pull customers away from the competition when they realized how much more they could save by switching to 366 Solar.

"We can launch yesterday," Harold stated.

"We're not going to do that," Emily replied.

Harold huffed. "And why not?"

"We're not ready."

Tyler leaned back in his chair. *I wonder how she's going to get him to understand that?*

"What if the app crashes?"

Harold waved his hand. "It's not going to do that. My team is too good." Harold had full confidence in what they had done. He had delegated the tasks to ensure they were tackled by the individual with the correct skills. "We have to launch. Otherwise, the competition will beat us to it." *Doesn't she understand?*

Emily smiled. She was reminded of the conversation she had with Paul. "I see what you're getting at. You're looking at the big picture and see that we have to get it on the market or the competition will beat us to it."

"Exactly!"

Now I have to get him to focus on the details. "Ever heard of the saying, what can go wrong, will go wrong?"

Harold took a second to digest that. He nodded. "Murphy's Law."

"Exactly. I know you see it as an impasse or me being stubborn, but my job is to ensure we create the best experience possible." Emily appreciated the drive and ambition Harold brought and she wanted him to understand that. "And unless we go through all the things that could go wrong, no matter how unlikely, we're not ready. I want to launch, too. I want everyone to experience the product you created, but at the right time and place. I hope you can understand that."

Harold nodded. He realized Emily wasn't trying to be an obstacle. That she wanted what he wanted. They had just been expressing it differently. "Yeah, I get what you're saying."

"Regardless, we can still present it at the meeting on Friday."

Tyler frowned. "It's getting close."

"I know," Emily replied.

Harold looked at both of them. "The university bid is a good move for us."

Well, she thought *At least I know which way he'll vote. I still need to know more.* She looked over to Tyler and saw that he shared her concern.

WORKING TOGETHER

These differing styles can not only work together, they can also complement each other's strengths and compensate for their own shortcomings.

In this case, Emily was able to help Harold understand the risk in launching the app prematurely. They realized they wanted the same thing, but just had to modify the way they sought to achieve it.

WHEN A SAFETY STYLE MEETS A SAFETY STYLE

As we've seen, Safety Styles tend to be calm and patient people. Because of this, when they work together there is little chance of conflict.

Their challenge is that they are not usually risk takers, so they may have difficulty asserting their needs and in making choices. When confronted with unfamiliar territory, they may grow uncomfortable and not want to make a decision. They tend to avoid confrontation and may give in to demands in order to keep the peace.

MEET THE PEOPLE

Name	Role	Communication Style	Motivation
Emily Reed	Chief Experience Officer	Supporter	Safety
Trisha Mitchell	Human Resources	Investigator	Safety
Danielle Edmonds	Executive Assistant	Blend	

WEDNESDAY

Danielle shut down her computer with a sigh. It was late, but she usually enjoyed being the last one to leave. This week, however, had taken its toll on everybody. Every department was focused on Friday's meeting. *And with good reason,* she thought. It represented the next step to take them from being just another solar energy company to becoming a major player. *But like everything, it has its risks.*

She thought about how it had affected the people she worked with. Danielle liked to compare her job to being an ambassador to the United Nations. Different people with different languages, all with the same common goal. That's how she saw her colleagues' Communication Styles. *They try so hard to make themselves understood that they forget to try to understand each other instead.*

She stood up and was making her way out when she heard conversation coming from Emily Reed's office. *That's odd,* she thought. I*t's rare for her to have to stay after hours.*

Inside her office, Emily was talking things over with Trisha Mitchell from Human Resources. Emily loved working with Trisha. They saw eye to eye on a lot of things and Emily could always count on her when she needed to vent. And this week had been particularly stressful. The action meeting for the Alta California bid was two days away.

Trisha Mitchell was a meticulous and ordered person. She loved her job and was always looking for ways to keep the company moving harmoniously. She was worried about the changes the Alta California bid would cause at 366 Solar. It was an ambitious move and potentially good for the company, but it was her job to look at the fine details. It would represent more work for the current employees. She might lose some people. She would also have to find new talent. And Paul wanted all of that in writing for the meeting on Friday. It was keeping her up at night.

The worst part was that she sometimes found herself at a loss when trying to communicate with Paul or even Harold. It was much easier to talk to Emily about these things.

"What if we ask Paul to postpone the meeting?"

"I don't know if that would happen. He's pretty set on it.

"I'd like more time."

They heard a knock on the door. Danielle's voice vibrated through the glass. "Staying late?"

"Danielle," Emily said. "Come on in."

Danielle entered and saw the worry on their faces. "What's the problem?"

Trisha sighed. If there was one person she could always count on to understand, it was Danielle. Her style seemed to blend effortlessly with everyone else's. "The Alta California bid. I'm worried. I don't think there's enough time to draft what Paul wants. I think he's jumping the gun."

Emily chimed in, "I've had that exact same conversation with him already."

"You don't think we're ready?" Danielle asked. She suspected what the answer might be. Whatever it was, though, Danielle knew she had to communicate what Paul wanted. It was essential for the company.

HERE'S WHAT'S HAPPENING

Safety Styles are detail oriented and committed to following norms and regulations.

During times of chaos, they can feel overwhelmed. Safety Styles like people and tend to avoid rocking the boat. Because of this, they can sometimes benefit from consulting with someone else who is more comfortable taking risks.

THINK ABOUT THIS

What can Danielle do to help with this situation?

LET'S TRY THAT AGAIN

Danielle shut down her computer with a sigh. It was late, but she usually enjoyed being the last one to leave. This week, however, had taken its toll on everybody. Every department was focused on Friday's meeting. *And with good reason,* she thought. It represented the next step to take them from being just another solar energy company to becoming a major player. *But like everything, it has its risks.*

She thought about how it had affected the people she worked with. Danielle liked to compare her job to being an ambassador to the United Nations. Different people with different languages, all with the same common goal. That's how she saw her colleagues' Communication Styles. *They try so hard to make themselves understood that they forget to try to understand each other instead.*

She stood up and was making her way out when she heard conversation coming from Emily Reed's office. *That's odd,* she thought. I*t's rare for her to have to stay after hours.*

Inside her office, Emily was talking things over with Trisha Mitchell from Human Resources. Emily loved working with Trisha. They saw eye to eye on a lot of things and Emily could always count on her when she needed to vent. And this week had been particularly stressful. The action meeting for the Alta California bid was two days away.

Trisha Mitchell was a meticulous and ordered person. She loved her job and was always looking for ways to keep the company moving harmoniously. She was worried about the changes the Alta California bid would cause at 366 Solar. It was an ambitious move and potentially good for the company, but it was her job to look at the fine details. It would represent more work for the current employees. She might lose some people. She would also have to find new talent. And Paul wanted all of that in writing for the meeting on Friday. It was keeping her up at night.

The worst part was that she sometimes found herself at a loss when trying to communicate with Paul or even Harold. It was much easier to talk to Emily about these things. "What if we ask Paul to postpone the meeting?"

"I don't know if that would happen. He's pretty adamant.

"I'd like more time."

They heard a knock on the door. Danielle's voice vibrated through the glass. "Staying late?"

"Danielle," Emily said. "Come on in."

Danielle entered and saw the worry on their faces. "What's the problem?"

Trisha sighed. If there was one person she could always count on to understand, it was Danielle. Her style seemed to blend effortlessly with everyone else's. "The Alta California bid. I'm worried. I don't think there's enough time to draft what Paul wants. I think he's jumping the gun."

Emily chimed in, "I've had that exact same conversation with him already."

"You don't think we're ready?" Danielle asked. She suspected what the answer might be. Whatever it was, though, Danielle knew she had to communicate what Paul wanted. It was essential for the company.

"No, I don't," Trisha replied. "There's no way for me to gauge how many new hires we'll need. I'm not even sure the bid is right for where we are right now. The added stress might cause us to lose workers."

"I understand your concern. And I can see how you may think that Paul doesn't care. He doesn't always communicate caring, but I think he's working on it."

"That's true," Emily said. "It's been easier to talk with him lately."

"To be honest, I feel stuck," Trisha said. "I can't move backward because there's not time and I don't know how to move forward."

"Is there anything you think could help you?"

Trisha looked toward Emily. They had discussed an idea, but were hesitant to run it by Paul.

"What if ran a survey on the health of the organization?" Trisha asked. "It would give us a view of what everybody feels. What the company as a whole is thinking."

The idea seemed like a good one to Danielle. "I think that could work. We don't have time before Friday, but it would help to have that information in hand if we decide to move forward with the bid. I'll run it by Paul in the morning."

Trisha smiled. "Thank you. I don't think this company could manage without you."

"I second that," Emily said.

Danielle shook her head. "Nonsense. I'm glad I could help."

BRINGING OUT THE BEST IN EVERYONE

Safety Styles are loyal people and strive to create a harmonious environment. As they seek to maintain the peace, they can benefit from consulting with a more confrontational style.

Emily Reed and Trisha Mitchell realized the benefit of consulting with those they trusted.

ORDER STYLE WITH PEOPLE STYLE

Order Styles lean toward planning ahead and following deadlines and schedules.

On the contrary, People Styles tend to focus on spur of the moment ideas and are not afraid to take risks. These differences present many opportunities for potential conflict as shown in this illustration.

MEET THE PEOPLE

Name	Role	Communication Style	Motivation
Barbara Cole	Marketing Director	Promoter	People
Tyler Hughes	Chief Financial Officer	Analyzer	Order

THURSDAY

Tyler knocked on Barbara's door. Her assistant was nowhere to be seen, which was already starting to irk him. This wasn't how things should be done. Tyler looked at his watch and sighed in frustration. He had a busy day ahead and couldn't afford to fall behind this early.

Then he heard someone call his name. He turned to find Barbara walking toward him. She had a big smile on her face. "You're not looking for me are you?"

Of course I'm looking for you! Why else would I be outside your door? "You're late," he said.

"Yes, I am," she replied. She leaned in for a quick hug and Tyler responded half-heartedly.

I swear Barbara lives in a different time zone than the rest of us. "Do you have those reports for the millennial campaign?"

"What reports?"

"I sent you an email yesterday."

"My inbox has been flooded." *Doesn't he know emails are terrible for communication,* Barbara thought to herself. "Why didn't you just pop in and see me? You know I'm always available."

It bothered Tyler that she treated his attempts at communication so dismissively. He had neither the time nor the inclination to simply "pop" into her office. *She can be so unprofessional at times.* He found himself thinking again that this was not how things should be done.

"We talked about this on Tuesday."

"I'm still getting people's opinions it."

"You can't talk about things forever. Some of us have deadlines to keep," he said.

"It's just a deadline, Tyler. They can always be moved back."

No, he thought. *That's not how it works.* "I don't think you understand—

Why is he so concerned about this? Doesn't he know I'll get it done?

"Oh! That reminds me, I've got to submit the press release on the prototype. It's ready. Do you think the Alta California people will like it? How should we present it to them? I wonder if we should do a press conference? I mean, only if we go through with the bid, of course."

Barbara's rambling was suddenly threatening to give Tyler a headache.

HERE'S WHAT'S HAPPENING

A People Style communicator's conversation can sometimes seem like an inner train of thought spoken aloud.

Because of this, the Order Style may dismiss it as unprofessional. People Styles also tend to ignore failures or shortcomings, which may prove frustrating for the Order Style.

THINK ABOUT THIS

How can Tyler improve his efforts to communicate with Barbara?

An Order Style should also make an effort to recognize the People Style's creativity and try not to confine them to schedules or regulations.

LET'S TRY THAT AGAIN

Tyler knocked on Barbara's door. Her assistant was nowhere to be seen, which was already starting to irk him. This wasn't how things should be done. Tyler looked at his watch and sighed in frustration. He had a busy day ahead and couldn't afford to fall behind this early.

Then he heard someone call his name. He turned to find Barbara walking toward him. She had a big smile on her face. "You're not looking for me are you?"

Of course I'm looking for you! Why else would I be outside your door? "You're late," he said.

"Yes, I am," she replied. She leaned in for a quick hug and Tyler responded half-heartedly.

I swear Barbara lives in a different time zone than the rest of us. "Do you have those reports for the millennial campaign?"

"What reports?"

"I sent you an email yesterday."

"My inbox has been flooded." *Doesn't he know emails are terrible for communication,* Barbara thought to herself. "Why didn't you just pop in and see me? You know I'm always available."

It bothered Tyler that she treated his attempts at communication so dismissively. He had neither the time nor the inclination to simply "pop into" her office. *She can be so unprofessional at times.* He found himself thinking again that this was not how things should be done.

"We talked about this on Tuesday."

"I'm still getting people's opinions on it."

"You can't talk about things forever. Some of us have deadlines to keep," he said.

"It's just a deadline, Tyler. They can always be moved back."

No, he thought. *That's not how it works.* "I don't think you understand—

Why is he so concerned about this? Doesn't he know I'll get it done?

"Oh! That reminds me, I've got to submit the press release on the prototype. It's ready. Do you think the Alta California people will like it? How should we present it to them? I wonder if we should do a press conference? I mean, only if we go through with the bid, of course."

Barbara's rambling was suddenly threatening to give Tyler a headache.

"Barbara, I understand where you're trying to go, but can we focus on something else here?"

His words brought her back down to earth. "What is it?"

"The meeting is tomorrow. We can't move it. We can't reschedule it. I would like to have the data on the marketing efforts for millennials. If we go through with the bid, it would prove useful to implement your idea."

The compliment made Barbara smile. "Well, the thing is, I just can't have it ready tomorrow. I have other things in line and it's going to be difficult."

Tyler appreciated her honesty. "I understand that. Let's set aside some time next week. I can handle the numbers and set a schedule up. Once we have it ready, you can present it to Paul."

Barbara nodded. "I'm going to write it down in my agenda. Make you proud of me and everything."

Tyler smiled. "I'm already proud of the work you do."

"Thank you. That means a lot."

Tyler nodded. "I'll see you at the meeting tomorrow," he said.

"I wouldn't miss it for the world."

Tyler turned around and headed back to his office. Despite Barbara's cheerful nature, the meeting still loomed ahead.

BRINGING OUT THE BEST IN EVERYONE

People Styles sometimes prefer to move on to new projects without fine-tuning their last. This can prove frustrating for the Order Styles.

However, by merging their detail-oriented nature with the spontaneous creativity of the People Style, they can become a formidable team. Tyler was able to understand and appreciate Barbara's efforts while setting limits and boundaries that would help the overall project.

WHEN AN ORDER STY MEETS AN ORDER STYLE

Order Styles like to have control over their work and work environments. This desire for control can lead them to demand high work standards from themselves and from others.

While developing a plan of action, they can come into conflict with each other. When in conflict, neither of them will be inclined to back off to end a disagreement.

MEET THE PEOPLE

Name	Role	Communication Style	Motivation
Stacy O'Sullivan	Chief Operating Officer	Solver	Order
Tyler Hughes	Chief Financial Officer	Analyzer	Order
Danielle Edmonds	Executive Assistant	Blend	

THURSDAY

Tyler had cleared everything on his agenda for the day. *Well, almost everything,* he thought. He had a meeting with Stacy O'Sullivan, 366 Solar's Chief Operating Officer and Paul's right hand. Together, the two had gone into that garage with an idea and come out with a product. Paul's drive combined with her ability to plan ahead and to create and implement solutions had brought 366 Solar to where it was today.

She and Tyler didn't always see eye to eye, which had caused some conflict along the way. He suspected this might be one of those times. He had been meaning to bring something to her attention and the recent meeting between Emily Reed and Harold Dunn had confirmed it.

Stacy waited for Tyler to show up. She suspected she knew the reason he wanted to meet with her. *He can be so stubborn sometimes. Let's see how this plays out.* Her intercom squawked. It was Danielle letting her know that Tyler was here to see her. She told her to let him in.

Tyler stepped into Stacy's office. She nodded to him. "Tyler. Have a seat?" After his run-in with Barbara, he had to admit he appreciated Stacy's style of communication. It acknowledged his presence while respecting his space. *I hope the civility lasts,* he thought.

"You wanted to talk about something? It's not about the meeting tomorrow is it?"

"In a way. I met with Emily and Harold on the app this week. During that meeting I realized that it may not be in the best interest of the company for the IT department to report to me at all."

This wasn't what she was expecting. *What's his game here,* she wondered. *Is he trying to get out of responsibilities?* "Explain."

"My goals are to hit numbers and control spending. Harold's goal is to spend money. We're at complete odds. It's not working out."

"What do you propose?"

"We should shift the management of IT over to you."

"Because you don't want his spending to affect your year-end bonus? Or do you want to eliminate the responsibilities of having to manage or drive it?"

Tyler realized that she had missed his point completely. *How do I get her to understand me?*

HERE'S WHAT'S HAPPENING

Both Order Styles have a strong desire for control and must make an effort to listen to and accept the ideas of others. They tend to avoid showing weakness and strive to prove their competence. For them to work together successfully, they have to make an effort to avoid placing blame too early.

LET'S TRY THAT AGAIN

Tyler had cleared everything on his agenda for the day. Well, almost everything, he thought. He had a meeting with Stacy O'Sullivan, 366 Solar's Chief Operating Officer and Paul's right hand. Together, the two had gone into that garage with an idea and come out with a product. Paul's drive combined with her ability to plan ahead and to create and implement solutions had brought 366 Solar to where it was today.

She and Tyler didn't always see eye to eye, which had caused some conflicts along the way. He suspected this might be one of those times. He had been meaning to bring something to her attention and the recent meeting between Emily Reed and Harold Dunn had confirmed it.

Stacy waited for Tyler to show up. She suspected she knew the reason he wanted to meet with her. *He can be so stubborn sometimes. Let's see how this plays out.* Her intercom squawked. It was Danielle letting her know that Tyler was here to see her. She told her to let him in.

Tyler stepped into Stacy's office. She nodded to him. "Tyler. Have a seat?" After his run-in with Barbara, he had to admit he appreciated Stacy's style of communication. It acknowledged his presence while respecting his space. *I hope the civility lasts,* he thought.

"You wanted to talk about something? It's not about the meeting tomorrow is it?"

"In a way. I met with Emily and Harold on the app this week. During that meeting I realized that it may not be in the best interest of the company for the IT department to report to me at all."

This wasn't what she was expecting. *What's his game here,* she wondered. *Is he trying to get out of responsibilities?* "Explain."

"My goals are to hit numbers and control spending. Harold's goal is to spend money. We're at complete odds. It's not working out."

"What do you propose?"

"We should shift the management of IT over to you."

"Because you don't want his spending to affect your year-end bonus?"

Tyler saw that she had missed the point. *How do I get her to understand me?* Then, he realized something. *I don't. I have to make myself better understood.*

"I think I may have expressed myself incorrectly," Tyler stated. Stacy had been set to argue, but this comment defused her somewhat.

"How so?" she asked.

"The IT department's job is to act as a change agent. And we both know Harold does a pretty good job of that by himself."

Stacy chuckled. "Yes, he sure does."

"As it stands, there's a conflict of interest. He has to support us with the creation and application of technology which, at the end of the day, means spending more money.

Stacy saw where he was going with this. "But if we change the management of IT over to me, you avoid the conflict of interest when it comes to controlling that money."

"Yes, Harold's job and purpose would be much better served if I weren't constantly undercutting him."

"It'll enable IT to develop its full potential as a change agent. Especially now with the potential bid for Alta California." Stacy realized they weren't at odds. They were actually working toward the same goals.

BRINGING OUT THE BEST IN EVERYONE

Order Styles work best together when working parallel to each other rather than collaborating. When conflict arises, they should be aware of how they can utilize their unique strengths and pursue a policy of divide and conquer with regard to responsibilities.

WHEN ALL THE STYLES MEET

Corporations, as well as any human endeavor that numbers more than one, involve people working together. In a company, this labor should be directed toward a common goal.

That goal has been pursued by the different characters throughout these stories. We've seen how the differing styles of each member of the 366 Solar team have resulted in both conflict and resolution.

Now it's time for the final meeting and a decision.

Name	Role	Communication Style	Motivation
Paul Morgan	CEO	Doer	Action
Stacy O'Sullivan	Chief Operating Officer	Solver	Order
Tyler Hughes	Chief Financial Officer	Analyzer	Order
Danielle Edmonds	Executive Assistant	Blend	
Harold Dunn	Chief Technical Officer	Motivator	Action
Emily Reed	Chief Experience Officer	Supporter	Safety

FRIDAY

Paul stood before the window in his office. He thought about how far the company had come. *Now, we can take a big step forward. But I need everybody on board.* He heard a knock on his door and then Danielle's voice.

"Meeting's set to start, Paul."

Paul chuckled. "Yeah, on my way." He didn't know what he would do without her. She was the glue that kept everyone 366 Solar together. He was about to leave the office when he reached for his jacket. *That conference room is always chilly.*

Meanwhile, Emily rifled through the papers on her desk. She'd studied the proposal so much she could probably quote most of it by heart. *And yet, I still can't make a decision. It's a huge undertaking. We could lose so much.*

She stood up and gathered the papers. She had a meeting with the rest of the board in five minutes and there was no use in delaying any longer. Emily left her office, doubt still lingering in her mind.

Stacy and Harold walked together toward the conference room. She had just informed him of her discussion with Tyler yesterday. It had brought a smile to his lips and some worry to Stacy. *I'll let him loose and see what he comes up with, but I'll rein him in if I have to.*

Tyler Hughes was already in the conference room. He had been reviewing the numbers in his head for quite a while now. The proposal was very interesting, no doubt about it. *It's good. Paul did good here. But the risk! We're stretched pretty thin right now. Where do we even get the money?* Tyler shuddered at the thought.

The door opened and Emily walked into the room. "Tyler. How're you doing?"

"Not bad. Looking over these numbers. I'm sure you've done the same."

"Yeah. Is it just me or has it kept you up at night?"

Tyler smiled. "Good to know I'm not the only one."

Stacy and Harold came in together.

"Hello, everybody," Harold said.

"Looks like we're just waiting on Paul now," Stacy said.

There was an awkward silence in the room. It wasn't broken until Paul and Danielle entered. She took a seat while Paul strode to the head of the table.

"Why is it always so cold in here?"

"It's been that way since we moved into the building," Emily replied. "I think it's a duct issue."

"Oh well," Paul said. "So, what do you think? Yes or no?"

"Yes, yes and yes," Harold said.

"Well, that takes care of one," Paul said with a grin.

Emily and Tyler immediately shared a look.

You'd think I'd be used to his brusque manner by now, Emily thought. "The truth is, I just don't know, Paul."

"Tyler?"

"I feel the same way."

Paul took a deep breath. *Time to break down some barriers,* he thought. "You can't deny it's a fantastic opportunity."

It could be, Emily thought. *It really could.* "The university comprises so many demographics, though, so many factors to consider, so much to—"

"Exactly! It's a great opportunity! Think of all we'll gain when they realize the benefit of our panels. It's a dream come true."

Emily felt sick to her stomach. "The social backlash could be huge."

"Come on, Emily! Tyler? Can you jump in here?"

Tyler had done the numbers. Over and over again. It was time to make his decision. "I think it's too ambitious. Are we really ready for something like this? I want to do another feasibility study."

"You've already done two of them. I think that's enough."

Tyler shook his head. "I need more information, Paul."

Emily jumped in with what she had discussed with Trisha the night before. "How does the rest of the company feel about this?"

Stacy had been quiet but now decided to chime in. "You're stalling for time, Emily. You know that."

"I only want to avoid risk," Emily said.

"And so do I," Tyler added.

"No risk, no reward." *And that's exactly the problem here,* Paul thought. *How do I get them to see the reward?*

HERE'S WHAT'S HAPPENING

The primary goal of communication among the styles is to understand others more than to be understood. The lack of understanding can result in conflict as we've seen throughout the previous stories as well as this final one.

Let's see how they can work together to ensure a more harmonious work environment while moving forward to achieve the company's goals.

LET'S TRY THAT AGAIN

Paul stood before the window in his office. He thought about how far the company had come. *Now, we can take a big step forward. But I need everybody on board.* He heard a knock on his door and then Danielle's voice.

"Meeting's set to start, Paul."

Paul chuckled. "Yeah, on my way." He didn't know what he would do without her. She was the glue that kept everybody at 366 Solar together. He was about to leave the office when he reached for his jacket. *That conference room is always chilly.* Meanwhile, Emily rifled through the papers on her desk. She'd studied the proposal so much she could probably quote most of it by heart. *And yet, I still can't make a decision. It's a huge undertaking. We could lose so much.*

She stood up and gathered the papers. She had a meeting with the rest of the board in five minutes and there was no use in delaying any longer. Emily left her office, doubt still lingering in her mind.

Stacy and Harold walked together toward the conference room. She had just informed him of her discussion with Tyler yesterday. It had brought a smile to his lips and some worry to Stacy. *I'll let him loose and see what he comes up with, but I'll rein him in if I have to.*

Tyler Hughes was already in the conference room. He had been reviewing the numbers in his head for quite a while now. The proposal was very interesting, no doubt about it. *It's good. Paul did good here. But the risk! We're stretched pretty thin right now. Where do we even get the money?* Tyler shuddered at the thought.

The door opened and Emily walked into the room. "Tyler. How're you doing?"

"Not bad. Looking over these numbers. I'm sure you've done the same."

"Yeah. Is it just me or has it kept you up at night?"

Tyler smiled. "Good to know I'm not the only one."

Stacy and Harold came in together.

"Hello, everybody," Harold said.

"Looks like we're just waiting on Paul now," Stacy said.

There was an awkward silence in the room. It wasn't broken until Paul and Danielle entered. She took a seat while Paul strode to the head of the table.

"Why is it always so cold in here?"

"It's been that way since we moved into the building," Emily replied. "I think it's a duct issue."

"Oh well," Paul said. "So, what do you think? Yes or no?"

"Yes, yes and yes," Harold said.

"Well, that takes care of one," Paul said with a grin.

Emily and Tyler immediately shared a look.

You'd think I'd be used to his brusque manner by now, Emily thought. "The truth is, I just don't know, Paul."

"Tyler?"

"I feel the same way."

Paul took a deep breath. *Time to break down some barriers,* he thought. "You can't deny it's a fantastic opportunity."

It could be, Emily thought. *It really could.* "The university comprises so many demographics, though, so many factors to consider, so much to—"

"Exactly! It's a great opportunity! Think of all we'll gain when they realize the benefit of our panels. It's a dream come true."

Emily felt sick to her stomach. "The social backlash could be huge."

"Come on, Emily! Tyler? Can you jump in here?"

Tyler had done the numbers. Over and over again. It was time to make his decision. "I think it's too ambitious. Are we really ready for something like this? I want to do another feasibility study."

"You've already done two of them. I think that's enough."

Tyler shook his head. "I need more information, Paul."

Emily jumped in with what she had discussed with Trisha the night before. "How does the rest of the company feel about this?"

Stacy had been quiet but now decided to chime in. "You're stalling for time, Emily. You know that."

"I only want to avoid risk," Emily said.

"And so do I," Tyler added.

"No risk, no reward." *And that's exactly the problem here,* Paul thought. *How do I get them to see the reward?*

"Emily, I always appreciate what you bring to the table, but sometimes we have to leap before we look."

Emily shook her head. "You're wagering the future of this company."

"Emily's right," Tyler said. "We'd need to take out a massive loan just to meet the demand. What if we can't repay it?"

Paul was about to fire off a response when he thought of something else. "When did we become all about the line?" The question made Tyler frown.

"Without a bottom line, there's no company," Tyler replied.

" I disagree. A company is more than just numbers in a bank. A company is a vision. We've worked hard to build this company. And, yes, now we have shares and shareholders when before all we had were benches in my garage."

Stacy smiled at the distant yet fond memory."

Paul continued. "That vision is about to come to fruition. This is our opportunity to do something big, to make a statement." Paul saw Tyler nodding along. *I think I've got him.* Emily, however, still had that frown. *She's a hard sell.*

"We'd have to secure a loan," Tyler said.

Emily was still conflicted. She could see that Tyler had been swayed. She wanted to please Paul but she also couldn't risk the future of the company.

"Thank you, Tyler," Paul said. "Emily?"

"But what if we fail?"

"Then we'll fail spectacularly."

"Paul!"

Tyler jumped in with a comment. "Well, according to Barbara, any publicity is good publicity."

Emily turned to face him. "Bankruptcy is not good publicity."

"No, you're right about that."

"Look, risk is unavoidable," Paul said. "I think that's a fact in any venture."

"Maybe."

"We can't avoid risk, Emily." Those words opened up a whole new train of thought for her. "Help me to mitigate the risk instead."

He's right, Emily thought. *We can't avoid risk forever.* "Well, I think I can do that."

Paul looked at everybody in the room. A sense of calm came over him. Everybody was on board.

"Thank you. All of you. There's nobody I trust more to move this company forward. I know we've had our issues, our disagreements, and our conflicts. We each may communicate in different ways, but we share the same vision. And I believe that's what makes this company so special."

When Good Styles Go Bad

COMMUNICATING WITH DIFFICULT PEOPLE

One of the things I hear frequently in my seminars is some version of "I work with Roger and he is impossible. He's so difficult that I try to avoid him when I can." Some people go on to explain that the person is so unpleasant that they are thinking of transferring to a different department or even quitting their job just to get away from them.

Other stories are not about work, but about personal and romantic relationships that are in crisis because either one or both of the people are "difficult."

Sometimes the story ends with the question: "Is it just me, or is this person really being difficult?" The answer is that, yes there really are difficult people in our lives that we have to communicate with.

We all know from life experience that some people are easier to communicate and get along with than others. These people always seem to know what to say, have interesting stories, and are actually fun to talk to.

Then there are the people who are so unpleasant that just thinking about them makes you break into a sweat and you will do almost anything to avoid them.

While there are many reasons why people are difficult, we're going to take a look at some of the common difficult people types that are caused by extreme Communication Styles.

WHY PEOPLE BECOME DIFFICULT

There are dozens of reasons why people might become difficult, but they all come down to one explanation—It works for them in some way.

The bad behavior gets them something they want and while the communication strategy they are using may have bad side effects, over a period of time they have been rewarded for using it.

> *People become difficult because it's the best way that they can think of to get what they want.*

Years ago I began my seminars by asking the group if there were any questions. I still remember one man whose arm shot up like it was on a spring. "Yes," he said, "I have a question. Why is my wife yelling at me all the time?"

The class laughed nervously, but I already knew the answer.

She was constantly yelling at him because she didn't think he was listening (she was probably right) and she thought that if she talked louder he would hear her better and listen. It was a flawed communication strategy, of course, because no matter how loudly she talked he still didn't listen to her.

But it was the best solution she could come up with and sometimes it worked so she kept using it.

When you think about it you can see that she was trying to get something positive out of her behavior, which was to get her husband to listen to her. The problem is that she was using bad behavior to try to get a good (from her perspective) result.

I'm sure that both the husband and the wife in this relationship would describe each other as being "difficult." And they would both be right.

EXTREME COMMUNICATION STYLES

There are dozens of types of bad behaviors and difficult people. We could spend days studying them all, so to keep it manageable I'm going to concentrate on a few of the common difficult behaviors that are caused by Communication Styles and motivations being taken to an extreme.

On the next pages we'll continue with the story about the employees of 366 Solar. Some of the characters will be new and some of them will be people you have already met, but their behaviors will have become difficult because their motivations have gone to an extreme.

It takes just a small change in a motivation to create a difficult person. Here are some examples:

Motivation	Changed Motivation	Resulting Difficult Behaviors
Action	Control	Bully, Expert, Time Bomb
People	Attention or Approval	Expert, Time Bomb
Safety	Appreciation or Attention	Silent Type, The Indecisive, Yes Person
Order	Perfection	Naysayer, Silent Type, Whiner

These are some examples of how positive motivations can turn into negative motivations. When the desire for action turns into a need for control it can create a difficult person. Or when the desire for action is so strong that the person ignores all other considerations they can easily become a Bully who just charges ahead and tries to intimidate everyone in their path.

They still have the same basic motivation—action—but it has been taken to an extreme.

When the people motivation becomes an unhealthy need for attention or approval you probably don't want to be near this person whose communication has become all about them. There's nothing inherently unhealthy about wanting some attention or approval, but when it is taken to an extreme the person becomes difficult.

Some people use these difficult behaviors on as their primary strategy on a regular basis, and some only use them occasionally. Either way, you need to know how to be as effective as possible with each of them.

THE RESULTS YOU SHOULD EXPECT

Before I give you any specific strategies, here's what you can reasonably expect to accomplish when you set out to manage one of these difficult people.

YOU CAN'T "FIX" THEM

They probably aren't going to change, so don't expect them to and you won't be disappointed.

They've developed their difficult behavior strategies over a period of many years and it gives them positive rewards in some way. It's not realistic to think that you are going to be able to change or "fix" them no matter what you do.

Your objective should be to get the difficult person to stop doing their bad behavior with *you*. They may (and probably will) continue to do it with other people, but you should consider yourself successful if they stop doing it with you.

Even a reduction in the frequency or intensity of the bad behavior should be considered a success. They might even start to avoid *you* because you won't cooperate with them and reward their strategy.

So, let's define a successful outcome as any reduction in the pain that they cause for you—however it happens.

REMEMBER

I'm going to repeat a few points I made earlier because they are so important to your success in working with difficult people.

People do bad behaviors for good reasons (from their viewpoint).

In general, (not always) the bad behavior that you dislike so much gets them something they want. Your best plan is to get the difficult person to stop using their bad behavior to get what they want when they use it with *you*.

They may still use it with other people—your outcome is to stop them from doing it with *you*.

DO YOU STILL HAVE TO "STEP UP?"

This is another question people frequently ask me.

And the answer is yes. You still have to take responsibility for the outcome of the communication.

If you don't approach it with this attitude of responsibility you are a helpless victim doomed to endure whatever the difficult person does to you.

So, "Step up."

In these next stories we are going to meet some of the types of difficult people, but there are many more types that we won't be covering. Here's a process that you can use with any difficult behavior:

- Think: what is this person's motivation for doing this? What do they want? What do they gain?
- Think: how can I redirect them to get what they want in a better way?
- If they continue to use the difficult behavior with you, make sure that they don't get what they want from using the behavior when they do it with you.

The combination of stopping the existing behavior from getting them what they want and showing them how to get what they want using better behaviors is powerful and can be used to help you with almost any difficult person you encounter.

Now, let's rejoin the people of 366 Solar as they work to implement the contract with Alta California.

THE BIG BULLY

The motivation behind this type of bad behavior has its roots exclusively in Action; you won't see them motivated by anything else. They see themselves as extremely competent at getting things done and that's all they ever think about.

They push and cajole and run right over people in getting to their objective. This is an extreme result of the Action Style and if they are not careful in their behavior they can roll right over everybody.

Let's look in on a meeting between Russel Davis, the angel investor we met earlier and Tyler Hughes who is going to be the recipient of his Big Bully attack.

MEET THE PEOPLE

Name	Role	Communication Style	Motivation
Russel Davis	Angel Investor	Challenger	Action
Tyler Hughes	Chief Financial Officer	Analyzer	Order

Russell Davis headed to the meeting with Tyler Hughes with a clear sense of determination.

The deal with Alta California had invigorated him in a way he hadn't thought possible. *It's incredible what a couple of months can do,* Russell thought. The ambition that had always fueled him had grown and now he had his sights set on so much more. Which was exactly the reason he had set up the meeting with Tyler.

As Russell walked down the hallway, he thought about the changes that had overtaken 366 Solar. There were new faces that Trisha Mitchell, the head of HR, had brought in to move the project along. The company had moved to a larger building and people were still getting accustomed to their new offices. *Everything is moving right along. And I'm going to make sure it continues to do so.*

Tyler was one of those who was still getting used to the changes. The new conference room he was in was much bigger than their previous one and there were some unfamiliar faces among the staff that unnerved him.

He liked things to be nice and neat and in their place. It was almost overwhelming. And even though this was everything he'd ever wanted for the company, he sometimes found himself missing the good old days. *Those are long gone now,* he thought. The pressure from the Alta California deal had built up and he was really starting to feel it.

And now this meeting with Russell Davis. *I don't know how Paul manages him,* Tyler thought. The man was known for having an explosive temper and could be something of a bully. Still, he was an integral part of the company and they couldn't just get rid of him. Tyler wished that Paul or even Stacy could be here today. But they were overseeing the new production facility in Nevada

"Tyler!" Russell said as he burst into the new conference room. "How're those projections?"

Straight to the point, Tyler thought. *I hope he lets me get a word in edgewise.*

"Well, I have questions."

Russell was in full-fledged action mode so he waved the comment aside. "Oh, you always have questions. What I want to know is feasibility. Will the rest of the shareholders go along with it? Will Paul?"

Tyler shook his head. "We've just gotten the Alta California project into motion. Why would we want to move forward on something like this?" That something was a bid to supply solar panels for a major defense installation.

This was something that Russell had set into motion without letting anybody on the board know. *I know Paul won't be happy about this.*

Russell smiled. "Why should we move forward? Because we can. Because we should. Because it'll increase our market share."

"I'm not sure I agree."

"Well, I'm not sure you know anything about this part of the business. You're just here to crunch numbers."

The remark came as a shock to Tyler. *Whoa. That's out of line.* "It's my job to ask these questions."

Russell scoffed at him. "Are you saying no?"

"That's not what I'm saying. I just think that—"

"Are you saying no?"

"Well, I—"

"Stop!" Russell shouted as he stood up and started to pace across the room. "Your opinion isn't what I care about right now. Can we get the money? Just tell me that! Can we?"

The attack had left Tyler at a loss for words.

WHAT'S GOING ON HERE

In this story, Russell's extreme action motivation results in his becoming a Bully who just wants to steamroll over anything and everything Tyler could say. In his single minded focus to take action and get results, he really doesn't care about whether Tyler is right or whether he's hurt or offended.

This strategy has worked for Russell most of his life and unless Tyler manages to recognize the situation, it will work here as well.

What can Tyler do to stop the attack and avert the conflict?

LET'S TRY THAT AGAIN

Russell Davis headed to the meeting with Tyler Hughes with a clear sense of determination.

The deal with Alta California had invigorated him in a way he hadn't thought possible. *It's incredible what a couple of months can do,* Russell thought. The ambition that had always fueled him had grown and now he had his sights set on so much more. Which was exactly the reason he had set up the meeting with Tyler.

As Russell walked down the hallway, he thought about the changes that had overtaken 366 Solar. There were new faces that Trisha Mitchell, the head of HR, had brought in to move the project along. The company had moved to a larger building and people were still getting accustomed to their new offices. *Everything is moving right along. And I'm going to make sure it continues to do so.*

Tyler was one of those who was still getting used to the changes. The new conference room he was in was much bigger than their previous one and there were some unfamiliar faces among the staff that unnerved him.

He liked things to be nice and neat and in their place. It was almost overwhelming. And even though this was everything he'd ever wanted for the company, he sometimes found himself missing the good old days. *Those are long gone now,* he thought. The pressure from the Alta California deal had built up and he was really starting to feel it.

And now this meeting with Russell Davis. *I don't know how Paul manages him,* Tyler thought. The man was known for having an explosive temper and could be something of a bully. Still, he was an integral part of the company and they couldn't just get rid of him. Tyler wished that Paul or even Stacy could be here today. But they were overseeing the new production facility in Nevada

"Tyler!" Russell said as he burst into the new conference room. "How're those projections?"

Straight to the point, Tyler thought. *I hope he lets me get a word in edgewise.*

"Well, I have questions."

Russell was in full-fledged action mode so he waved the comment aside. "Oh, you always have questions. What I want to know is feasibility. Will the rest of the shareholders go along with it? Will Paul?"

Tyler shook his head. "We've just gotten the Alta California project into motion. Why would we want to move forward on something like this?" That something was a bid to supply solar panels for a major defense installation.

This was something that Russell had set into motion without letting anybody on the board know. *I know Paul won't be happy about this.*

Russell smiled. "Why should we move forward? Because we can. Because we should. Because it'll increase our market share."

"I'm not sure I agree."

"Well, I'm not sure you know anything about this part of the business. You're just here to crunch numbers."

The remark came as a shock to Tyler. *Whoa. That's out of line.* "It's my job to ask these questions."

Russell scoffed at him. "Are you saying no?"

"That's not what I'm saying. I just think that—"

"Are you saying no?"

"Well, I—"

"Stop!" Russell shouted as he stood up and started to pace across the room. "Your opinion isn't what I care about right now. Can we get the money? Just tell me that! Can we?"

The attack had left Tyler at a loss for words.

He knew that had to get through to Russell and make him realize that this was a bad idea. He took a deep breath. "Russell."

"Don't patronize me. I want to know now. Just do what I'm telling you!"

"Russell."

"I told you."

"Russell."

"What!"

"I'm not your enemy here."

Well, if he's not against me, Russell thought, *why won't he give me what I want?* He realized that he had been pacing back and forth and he stopped moving.

"Why won't you give me what I want?"

"Russell."

He sopped pacing sat down. "Fine. I'm listening."

I think I may have gotten through to him, Tyler thought.

"Russell, it's a great idea. And if we didn't have Alta California I wouldn't hesitate to move forward. The feasibility study works, but we're stretched thin as it is."

"You'll figure something out."

"Russell."

"How do I know you're right?"

Tyler did a double take. *What is wrong with him?* Tyler realized that this was a challenge to his authority and expertise. He had to stand his ground. "Russell, I have the utmost respect for what you brought to this company. You believed in us when nobody else did. But I have been here every single day since then, working to make our dream a reality. I have the expertise and Paul's implicit trust in these matters."

A dead silence hung in the air of the conference room. Tyler could sense something was brewing. *Is he going to explode?*

Russell stood up abruptly. "Expertise? Let's talk about expertise." He started to pace around the room again. "I've built and sold more companies than the years you've been alive."

Tyler sighed. *He's determined to just roll right over me. How do I stop him? Maybe I should just give in.* But he realized that if he did, Russell would continue to bully him every time. He couldn't encourage this type of behavior.

"Russell, your expertise is not in question. What is in doubt here is the project itself. It's not about you."

Russell stopped moving. "Okay. Thank you for your thoughts. I'll take them into consideration."

And with that, Russell turned and headed out of the conference room as quickly as he had entered.
Tyler leaned back in his chair and breathed a sigh of relief. *Well, I'm glad that worked. So far.*

HOW TO BE MOST EFFECTIVE WITH A BULLY

In this situation, Tyler didn't completely stop Russell's bad behavior, but he slowed it down. As a Bully, Russel is used to mowing everybody down in his path to get what he wants and he expected Tyler to just give in to him. Since it's always worked in the past, he'll continue to do it with other people but maybe not with Tyler as much.

Tyler stood his ground and remained assertive, while managing not to confront him directly. By doing so, Tyler was able to divert Russell from his single-minded goal and force him to back off and respect him.

He also used the pattern interrupt of repeating Russell's name over and over again to get him to stop demanding and pay attention to him for a minute.

Tyler didn't turn Russell into a passive puppy dog and he never will. However, he did begin to teach him that he won't respond to the Bully behavior and this makes it less likely that Russell will use it the next time they meet.

Here are some strategies for being more effective when you encounter a Bully:

- Stay assertive. If you back down from this bad behavior, they are going to run right over with you and learn that they can treat you however they want and have their own way.

- Don't confront them directly. If you do, they will double down and become even more aggressive. Repeatedly say their name until they pay attention. This will break their pattern and get them to stop their attack.

THE EXPERT

The difficult person known as an Expert can result from either a people or an action motivation.

There are two types of experts:

- The real experts who really are subject matter experts and know what they are talking about.
- The pretend experts who have no idea what they are talking about, basically make it up as they talk, and sound so authoritative that you think they might really know what they are talking about.

You can tell the difference between these two types because the subject matter expert will typically do their difficult behavior only when they are talking about their preferred subject. The pretend expert will feel free to be an expert in any subject that comes up.

MEET THE PEOPLE

Name	Role	Communication Style	Motivation
Barbara Cole	Marketing Director	Promoter	People
Grayson Orr	Public Relations Director	Persuader	People
Erin Clark	Marketing Assistant	Persuader	People
Danielle Edmonds	Executive Assistant	Blend	

Danielle Edmonds wished she could clone herself.

The flurry of activity since the Alta California deal had her all over the place. *If only HR would hurry up and get somebody to help me,* she thought.

Trisha Mitchell, the newly appointed head of HR, kept saying 'yes' but, so far, no result. *I should probably go have a talk with her soon.* But right now, she was in a meeting with Barbara Cole, Grayson Orr, and the newest member of the Marketing Department, Erin Clark.

Danielle had had her doubts about Erin. She seemed smart and had potential, but she was also fresh out of college. Which, according to Barbara, had been one of the reasons they hired her. They needed someone in touch with that age group, somebody who could help them improve their social media presence.

However, Danielle was worried about what she considered to be a serious flaw in the way Erin behaved in meetings.

Erin saw herself as an expert in her field and she would use any excuse to tell anybody about her massive Twitter following and her viral videos.

As she sat through the meeting, Erin found herself getting more and more anxious. *They're going about this all wrong,* she thought to herself. She felt like her expertise wasn't being consulted enough. When Barbara shifted the subject toward their new marketing campaign, Erin was eager to chime in.

"Let's talk about our new marketing campaign for Alta California," Barbara said.

Erin almost leaped out of her seat. "Yes. Please!"

Well, at least she's eager, Danielle thought.

"I've got a few questions about your proposal," Barbara said. "What studies have we done to further engage the students at Alta California?"

"Huh?" Erin said. "Studies? They're a waste of time."

"Excuse me? I wouldn't call them a waste of time. I'm just glad Tyler isn't in the room. You'd hear the same from him."

Erin stood up and shook her head. "Absolutely. A waste of time. And not only that but a waste of money. I already know exactly what they're looking for."

Does she? Danielle wondered. *She certainly doesn't know how to behave in a meeting.*

Erin realized that they just didn't know what they were talking about. And it was up to her to educate them on the subject. It was something she was comfortable with. In college she was always the smartest person in the room, smarter than her professors even. She never had any issues letting them know when they made a mistake.

Erin sighed. "Listen to me. I've got the followers to prove it. And my last video? Viral. Over a million views in less than a week. That should tell you all you need to know."

Danielle shook her head. *Even if she's right and has the right knowledge, she's going about it the wrong way. If we had a spotlight, it would shine bright on her right now. I wonder how Barbara is going to handle this?*

WHAT'S GOING ON HERE

Erin's motivation lies in People. However, as an Expert, she really cares more about Attention.

These difficult people tend to be aggressive and will often interrupt you and correct you in an effort to make sure you know how much of an expert they are.

They will tell you what you are doing is wrong and why you are doing it all wrong. The Expert is determined to impress everyone with their knowledge. Whether they are an expert in their subject matter or not, it is the way they approach things that makes them a difficult person.

What can Barbara Cole do to curb Erin's bad behavior?

LET'S TRY THAT AGAIN

Danielle Edmonds wished she could clone herself.

The flurry of activity since the Alta California deal had her all over the place. *If only HR would hurry up and get somebody to help me,* she thought.

Trisha Mitchell, the newly appointed head of HR, kept saying 'yes' but, so far, no result. *I should probably go have a talk with her soon.* But right now, she was in a meeting with Barbara Cole, Grayson Orr, and the newest member of the Marketing Department, Erin Clark.

Danielle had had her doubts about Erin. She seemed smart and had potential, but she was also fresh out of college. Which, according to Barbara, had been one of the reasons they hired her. They needed someone in touch with that age group, somebody who could help them improve their social media presence.

However, Danielle was worried about what she considered a serious flaw in the way Erin behaved in meetings.

Erin saw herself as an expert in her field and she would use any excuse to tell anybody about her massive Twitter following and her viral videos.

As she sat through the meeting, Erin found herself getting more and more anxious. *They're going about this all wrong,* she thought to herself. She felt like her expertise wasn't being consulted enough. When Barbara shifted the subject toward their new marketing campaign, Erin was eager to chime in.

"Let's talk about our new marketing campaign for Alta California," Barbara said.

Erin almost leaped out of her seat. "Yes. Please!"

Well, at least she's eager, Danielle thought.

"I've got a few questions about your proposal," Barbara said. "What studies have we done to further engage the students at Alta California?"

"Huh?" Erin said. "Studies? They're a waste of time."

"Excuse me? I wouldn't call them a waste of time. I'm just glad Tyler isn't in the room. You'd hear the same from him."

Erin stood up and shook her head. "Absolutely. A waste of time. And not only that but a waste of money. I already know exactly what they're looking for."

Does she? Danielle wondered. *She certainly doesn't know how to behave in a meeting.*

Erin realized that they just didn't know what they were talking about. And it was up to her to educate them on the subject. It was something she was comfortable with. In college she was always the smartest person in the room, smarter than her professors even. She never had any issues letting them know when they made a mistake.

Erin sighed. "Listen to me. I've got the followers to prove it. And my last video? Viral. Over a million views in less than a week. That should tell you all you need to know."

Danielle shook her head. *Even if she's right and has the right knowledge, she's going about it the wrong way. If we had a spotlight, it would shine bright on her right now. I wonder how Barbara is going to handle this?*

Barbara had hired Erin for this exact type of expertise. However, this bad behavior couldn't be tolerated. "First of all, I never said you didn't know."

"Thank you. Now, my plan is to—"

Barbara shook her head. "Hold on there." *She's getting ahead of herself. Even if she's right about her proposal, she needs to learn to ask the proper questions.* This was something Barbara had learned from Tyler Hughes. *I wonder if that's how he saw me?*

"What if we approach the demographic from a different angle?" Barbara asked. "What can we do that hasn't been done? I think some studies might help us there. What do you think of that?"

The questions interrupted Erin's train of thought for a moment, then she continued her attack. "Those are some interesting questions but more studies are a waste of resources! Everybody here is simply out of touch with this demographic."

"Let me ask you this then. Are we at the forefront of innovation? Have you looked at what others are doing?"

"No, but—"

"You don't think that might help?"

Erin found that Barbara's questions poked some holes in her certainty.

Barbara knew she wasn't going to win an argument with Erin. And she didn't want to. She just wanted to make sure she realized how people were expected to behave at 366 Solar. That her Expert attitude wouldn't get her far here.

"Listen," Barbara said. "I respect your expertise. It's one of the reasons we value you so much here. Will you consider this issue and let me know what you think? It may be the best approach for the company as a whole."

Erin thought about Barbara's questions for a second. Her concerns were legitimate and it was for the good of the company anyhow. "I'll think about what you said."

Barbara smiled.

For her part, Danielle couldn't be prouder of how Barbara had handled Erin. The situation could've gotten out of hand very easily. Erin brought a lot to the table, but her bad behavior couldn't be tolerated.

HOW TO BE MOST EFFECTIVE WITH AN EXPERT

Barbara was able to defuse the situation by raising questions that focused on getting Erin to think rather than on winning an argument.

Here are some tips about how to be more effective when dealing with an expert:

- Present ideas with respect. What this means is that you shouldn't challenge them directly.
- Make sure you're as knowledgeable as possible about the topic at hand. If they are a true expert, make sure you've e got your facts straight because they will challenge you on it.
- Use soft statements when addressing them. Start your sentences with softeners like "maybe" and "possibly."
- End them with "what do you think?" It makes the challenge less confrontational and sidesteps their motivation for attention. Softening things up makes what you are saying much more palatable to them.
- With the Expert, you're never going to win an argument so it's best not to try. The best thing to do is to ask them questions and slow them down to get them to think about other alternatives.

THE YES PERSON

The motivation behind this type of difficult person has its roots exclusively in Safety. This person will agree to everything all of the time regardless of whether or not they really think they can do it.

This can result in destructive consequences for this person and for those around them. They will answer any challenge and request with a "yes," but the truth is they have neither the time, the resources, nor the energy to do everything they agree to. They will take on too much work to avoid creating conflict but only end up letting others down.

MEET THE PEOPLE

Name	Role	Communication Style	Motivation
Trisha Mitchell	Human Resources	Investigator	Safety
Danielle Edmonds	Executive Assistant	Blend	

Trisha Mitchell clicked 'end' on her most recent Skype interview.

She shook her head and leaned back in her chair. *I could barely hear him,* she thought. *Still, he has a pretty impressive resume. I could bring him in for a personal interview.* She took the candidate's resume with the intention of placing it in the consider file. *Where did I put it?*

She usually had a state of controlled chaos in her office. But, lately, things had gotten really out of hand. The Alta California deal had presented her with a promotion to the head of Human Resources.

She had said 'yes' without even thinking about it. And now, she found that she was constantly on the phone vetting candidates, looking at resumes, and handling conflicts with the new hires. What had started out as an exciting project had quickly turned into a nightmare.

The requirements for the Alta California deal increased the pressure on her to find outstanding talent for the project. And it seemed like everybody needed her help. She had committed herself to everyone who had asked for her assistance. She had been on track for a while, but as the requests grew, so had her obligations.

Danielle headed toward Trisha's office with some reservation. She knew Trisha was probably swamped like everybody else at 366 Solar. However, she also had noticed that Trisha rarely let people know if she were having any problems. It was a good quality and one that had gotten her the promotion. But would the added responsibilities be too much for her?

Danielle found Trisha digging through a file cabinet in her office. "Hey, Trisha, how are you today?" She heard Trisha mumble something. "Trish?"

Trisha jumped in surprise. "Oh! Danielle! I didn't see you." She had been so lost in searching for the file that she hadn't heard Danielle come in.

"I wanted to talk to you about something. Have you got a minute?"

Trisha knew that she didn't, but she didn't want to disappoint Danielle. "Yes! Please. Sit down." She saw that the chairs in her office were stacked with paperwork. She hurried to clear some space for Danielle to sit down.

"Thanks," Danielle said as she took a seat. "Are you going to sit down?"

"Oh, sorry. Yes."

"I sent you an email last week. What do you think?"

"Um, could you remind me?"

"It was about hiring another executive assistant. You said you would look into it."

"Of course. Yes. I will."

"Do you have the time to do it? It looks like you're swamped with work."

"Oh, don't worry. I'll make it a top priority."

Danielle frowned. She had heard this before.

WHAT'S GOING ON HERE

The stressful environment of the Alta California deal has frazzled Trisha Mitchell.

Because her motivation is Safety, she does not want to disappoint anyone. This has caused her to say "yes" to every single request. By doing so, she has overcommitted herself and has caused conflict for those around her. What can Danielle do to help with the situation?

LET'S TRY THAT AGAIN

Trisha Mitchell clicked 'end' on her most recent Skype interview.

She shook her head and leaned back in her chair. *I could barely hear him,* she thought. *Still, he has a pretty impressive resume. I could bring him in for a personal interview.* She took the candidate's resume with the intention of placing it in the consider file. *Where did I put it?*

She usually had a state of controlled chaos in her office. But, lately, things had gotten really out of hand. The Alta California deal had presented her with a promotion to the head of Human Resources.

She had said 'yes' without even thinking about it. And now she found that she was constantly on the phone vetting candidates, looking at resumes, and handling conflicts with the new hires. What had started out as an exciting project had quickly turned into a nightmare.

The requirements for the Alta California deal increased the pressure on her to find outstanding talent for the project. And it seemed like everybody needed her help. She had committed herself to everyone who had asked for her assistance. She had been on track for a while, but as the requests grew, so had her obligations.

Danielle headed toward Trisha's office with some reservation. She knew that Trisha was probably swamped like everybody else at 366 Solar. However, she also had noticed that Trisha rarely let people know if she was having any problems. It was a good quality and one that had gotten her the promotion. But would the added responsibilities be too much for her?

Danielle found Trisha digging through a file cabinet in her office. "Hey, Trisha, how are you today?" She heard Trisha mumble something. "Trish?"

Trisha jumped in surprise. "Oh! Danielle! I didn't see you." She had been so lost in searching for the file that she hadn't heard Danielle come in.

"I wanted to talk to you about something. Have you got a minute?"

Trisha knew that she didn't, but she didn't want to disappoint Danielle. "Yes! Please. Sit down." She saw that the chairs in her office were stacked with paperwork. She hurried to clear some space for Danielle to sit down.

"Thanks," Danielle said as she took a seat. "Are you going to sit down?"

"Oh, sorry. Yes."

"I sent you an email last week. What do you think?"

"Um, could you remind me?"

"It was about hiring another executive assistant. You said you would look into it."

"Of course. Yes. I will."

"Do you have the time to do it? It looks like you're swamped with work."

"Oh, don't worry. I'll make it a top priority."

Danielle frowned. She had heard this before. "Are you sure?"

"Yes. Don't worry."

Danielle's first instinct was to call her out on the obvious lack of results. But she stopped herself from doing so.

Being so harsh to Trisha might have just the opposite of the desired effect. Danielle wanted to get her back on track without causing her to be embarrassed and feel like she had to defend her previous failures to deliver on promises.

It was true that she had overcommitted, but she *was* getting results, just not as fast as promised.

"Listen, Trisha, I wanted to thank you for the work you've put in since the Alta California deal. It's been stressful for all of us."

Trisha felt better instantly. "Nothing I can't handle." As she said this, though, Trisha couldn't help but feel the pressure closing around her even more.

"I know I said I needed your help in finding another executive assistant, but how about we put that off for a while." Danielle realized that while she may not get exactly what she wanted, she could get something. And at this point, getting Trisha back on track was much more important.

"Are you sure? I can absolutely take care of it."

"Let's schedule a meeting two weeks from now. We'll meet in the conference room on the 11th. At 9am."

"Yes. I can do that"

Danielle nodded. "I'll send you an email and you can confirm it there as well."

"Oh. Okay. That works for me."

Danielle knew that if there was something in writing, it would help Trisha to focus and get things done. "I'll talk to you then. And let me know if you need help with anything in the meantime."

Trisha nodded. "Thank you." She stood up and went back to attacking the chaos in the office. *I've got to get back on track. And I can't keep saying 'yes' to everybody and everything.*

As Danielle left, she considered the state of the department. *She's very hardworking but she needs to realize she can't bear the burden of everything on her own.* With that thought, Danielle chuckled. *Maybe I should learn that lesson, too.*

HOW TO BE MOST EFFECTIVE WITH A YES PERSON

Trisha's Safety motivation has pushed her toward the extreme of avoiding conflict at all cost.

She has said 'yes' to any and all demands of her time and responsibilities. Many times this just made things worse, but she really didn't know what else to do. Many things turned out okay, but she felt terrible when she disappointed someone.

Danielle recognized the situation and helped her to realize what was happening. She also avoided a direct conflict as it would only make things worse.

Here are some tips about how to be more effective when dealing with a Yes Person:

- This person needs you to be soft and kind, even if you are frustrated and don't feel like it.
- Set reasonable expectations for the Yes Person, but realize that they probably won't actually deliver everything they promise.
- Set interim goals and checkup frequently so that they know you are paying attention.
- If you really need a commitment, get it in writing. If they still don't deliver, confront them directly and let them know that you won't accept their non-performance.
- When you confront them, be as soft as possible while still being firm.

THE INDECISIVE

The Indecisive is motivated by Safety. When asked to do something, they often have trouble coming to a consensus or a decision.

MEET THE PEOPLE

Name	Role	Communication Style	Motivation
Paul Morgan	CEO	Doer	Action
Michael Taylor	Outside Contractor	Supporter	Safety
Danielle Edmonds	Executive Assistant	Blend	

Paul Morgan, the CEO of 366 Solar, was waiting for a conference call to begin.

He had Danielle Edmonds, his Executive Assistant, with him so that she could follow up on any decisions that were made during the call. They were scheduled to talk with Michael Taylor, the general contractor for their new manufacturing plant in Nevada. Paul was worried that they had fallen behind schedule and wanted to take stock of the situation.

Danielle looked at her watch. "What do you think the problem might be?"

"I don't know. He was meeting all of the previous deadlines. I was in constant communication with him, but for these past two weeks I haven't heard anything."

"Maybe he ran into some issues and didn't want to worry us."

"I can only hope that's the problem."

At his end, Michael was running to make it back to his office in time for his conference call with Paul and Danielle. The past few weeks had been hard on his nerves as well as his deadlines.

He'd been faced with shortages in both construction materials and workers. He'd been forced to make last minute decisions. *I'm not qualified to make them,* he thought. *But if I don't make them, we fall behind schedule. If I make the wrong one, then we also fall behind schedule. I just want to make the right ones.*

Michael made it to his office. He took a minute to catch his breath before sitting down. He dialed Paul's number and put him on speakerphone.

"Paul? It's Michael."

Finally, thought Paul. "Hey, Michael! I've got Danielle Edmonds here with me."

"Hi, Michael, How's it going?"

Michael was worried. If he brought Danielle in, then this conversation would take a lot longer than he wanted it to. "Hey, guys. It's going well. What's it like on your end?'

Paul glanced over at Danielle. *Is he stalling for time?* "Things are fine, Michael. We haven't heard from you in two weeks. We had constant updates before that. What's going on?"

Michael gulped. *Always to the point. I should get used to that.* "Uh, well, we had some issues with the construction workers."

Danielle was aghast. "Did they strike?"

"No, no, nothing like that. They just haven't been coming in to work."

"What?! So there's nobody on the site?

"A couple of them. Not the whole contingent."

"Did something happen to them?"

"Maybe. I can look into that."

"Well, why didn't you hire another company? You can do that."

"Yeah, maybe. I can, I mean, I have been looking into that as well."

Paul shook his head. "Is that the only issue?"

"No, we had some material shortages. That backed us up for another week."

"Could you have gotten it from somewhere else?"

"I think so. Is that something you would approve?"

Paul threw his hands up in the air. *What is going here? How can he be so indecisive? I need to take action. What am I going to do?*

WHAT'S GOING ON HERE

When the project ran into problems, Michael's natural Safety motivation resulted in indecision and finally paralysis. This naturally conflicts with Paul's action motivation.

How can Paul give him more certainty and safety and get the project back on track?

LET'S TRY THAT AGAIN

Paul Morgan, the CEO of 366 Solar, was waiting for a conference call to begin.

He had Danielle Edmonds, his Executive Assistant, with him. They were scheduled to talk with Michael Taylor, the general contractor for their new manufacturing plant in Nevada. Paul was worried that they had fallen behind schedule and wanted to take stock of the situation.

Danielle looked at her watch. "What do you think the problem might be?"

"I don't know. He was meeting all of the previous deadlines. I was in constant communication with him, but for these past two weeks I haven't heard anything."

"Maybe he ran into some issues and didn't want to worry us."

"I can only hope that's the problem."

At his end, Michael was running to make it back to his office in time for his conference call with Paul and Danielle. The past few weeks had been hard on his nerves as well as his deadlines.

He'd been faced with shortages in both construction materials and workers. He'd been forced to make last minute decisions. *I'm not qualified to make them,* he thought. *But if I don't make them, we fall behind schedule. If I make the wrong one, then we also fall behind schedule. I just want to make the right ones.*

Michael made it to his office. He took a minute to catch his breath before sitting down. He dialed Paul's number and put him on speakerphone.

"Paul? It's Michael."

Finally, thought Paul. "Hey, Michael! I've got Danielle Edmonds here with me."

"Hi, Michael, How's it going?"

Michael was worried. If he brought Danielle in, then this conversation would take a lot longer than he wanted it to. "Hey, guys. It's going well. What's it like on your end?'

Paul glanced over at Danielle. *Is he stalling for time?* "Things are fine, Michael. We haven't heard from you in two weeks. We had constant updates before that. What's going on?"

Michael gulped. *Always to the point. I should get used to that.* "Uh, well, we had some issues with the construction workers."

Danielle was aghast. "Did they strike?"

"No, no, nothing like that. They just haven't been coming in to work."

"What?! So there's nobody on the site?

"A couple of them. Not the whole contingent."

"Did something happen to them?"

"Maybe. I can look into that.

"Well, why didn't you hire another company? You can do that."

"Yeah, maybe. I can, I mean, I have been looking into that as well."

Paul shook his head. "Is that the only issue?"

"No, we had some material shortages. That backed us up for another week."

"Could you have gotten it from somewhere else?"

"I think so. Is that something you would approve?"

Paul threw his hands up in the air. *What is going here? How can he be so indecisive? I need to take action. What am I going to do?*

Danielle looked over and saw the frustration on Paul's face.

She could almost read his mind. *He doesn't get what's happening on the other end. But I do.* She could empathize with Michael's situation. He wants to get everything right, doesn't want to make a mistake, and it's paralyzed him. *I can see how that could happen to me.* Still, it wasn't the type of behavior that led to good decision making or business relationships. The construction project was in trouble right now and she had to correct it.

Danielle touched Paul on the shoulder. He looked over and recognized the determined look on her face. He realized that with her grasp of details she might be able to handle the situation better. He nodded and let her speak.

"Michael, I understand the situation. And I'm concerned, we're both concerned, about what you're going through."

They couldn't see him, but Michael nodded in response. He felt the tightness in his chest loosen a little as Danielle spoke.

"Tell me some of your concerns. What worries you about the materials?"

"Well, I'm worried about making our deadlines. The company we contracted for steel is usually on time, but now they're falling behind. I could look for another supplier but I feel most comfortable with somebody I know. There are always overseas manufacturers, in fact there's a company in Chile that could help, but, I don't know."

Danielle nodded. "I understand. What other concerns do you have?"

Paul leaned back and observed Danielle. He had learned so much from her and the rest of his team at 366 Solar. He found their different insights made certain situations easier to handle. *Like today. Without Danielle here, I probably would've scared Michael into submission and never gotten any real answers from him.*

Michael felt like the weight of the decision making had been lifted off his shoulders. Finally, someone who understood instead of demanding and yelling. "The workers are reliable. But they all got some sort of food poisoning. I didn't know what to do."

To Danielle, it looked like it had been one unfortunate incident after the other. They had swirled together into a perfect storm of indecisiveness on Michael's part. *What can I do to relieve it?* She looked over at Paul and raised an eyebrow.

Paul nodded at Danielle and leaned in toward the speaker. "Michael, Paul again. It looks like you had a series of unfortunate events."

Danielle smiled. *Did he read my mind?* She was amazed at how much Paul had changed. Since the Alta California deal, his ability to communicate had improved so much.

"Here's what we'll do. Send me a report of everything that's happened and what you think the options are. Danielle and I will review it and help you make a decision on both the workers and the materials."

Paul wasn't too happy about this approach. He didn't like to get bogged down by details. *But sometimes you had to modify your approach to get the job done,* he thought.

Michael smiled for the first time in weeks. "I can do that. Yeah. Thank you."

Danielle nodded. "Thank you for your hard work, Michael. Send that over to us today."

"I will," Michael replied. "Good-bye."

"Good-bye."

After the call ended, Danielle and Paul turned to face each other.

Paul nodded and smiled. "Thank you for stepping in there. You handled that well."

"*We* handled that well."

"Agreed. We'll take a look at what's going on. Then we're going to have to make a decision whether or not to keep Michael on as well."

"Yes. He's good, but this indecisive behavior could really set us back."

HOW TO BE MOST EFFECTIVE WITH AN INDECISIVE

Paul and Danielle were able to curb Michael's bad behavior through a series of concerted actions.

First of all, Paul delegated the task of managing Michael to Danielle who, as a Blend style, was better equipped to understand what Michael was going through. She provided Michael with the comfort zone he needed to get moving.

Both Paul and Danielle were patient enough to discover the issues at hand and ultimately help Michael come to the decisions he couldn't make on his own.

- Provide them with a comfort zone so that they know you're concerned about their situation. Do your best to understand their questions and concerns.
- Be patient and seek to discuss the conflict without forcing a decision. If you push too hard, they will become more paralyzed.
- Give them specific direction to help them to reach a consensus or decision. Provide options to choose from if necessary.

THE NAYSAYER

The motivation for the Naysayer is Order.

Because they want everything to be orderly and make sense, it can seem like they have a negative outlook on every issue. The Naysayer will ask a lot of questions and look for reasons why things won't work.

While this caution can be a valuable asset to an organization, it can also create a difficult person when it goes too far.

MEET THE PEOPLE

Name	Role	Communication Style	Motivation
Howard Dunn	Chief Technology Officer	Motivator	Action
Ray Phillips	Software Engineer	Solver	Order

Howard Dunn, the Chief Technology Officer for 366 Solar, was reviewing the performance of their new app.

The soon to launch application would keep track of the energy expenditure of each customer's solar array and use the mobile phone's camera to measure the intensity of the sunlight to calculate how much power each panel could generate.

He had held off on releasing it because of the Alta California bid. Now that they were well underway with that project, he was supervising putting the app through the final testing phase.

Everything looks good, he thought. He was glad he had listened to Emily Reed. She had been right about not launching earlier. Since then, he had uncovered some flaws that, while not fatal, would have detracted from the user's experience. Which was exactly what Emily had stressed. *I'm glad she found a way to get through my tunnel vision.*

As he ran the app through its final benchmark, he noticed a glitch on one of the screens. *Hmm,* he thought. *That won't look good. And Emily will not be happy either.* He stood up and headed over to see his group of engineers about the issue.

Ray Phillips was one of those engineers. Since the Alta California deal had gone through, he had been brought on board to help with the programming load. He had been working on the application full time for weeks, including staying late and working weekends.

Even with all of the extra time, Ray wasn't happy about the situation. The quality of the work being done was simply not up to what he considered to be the proper standard. *Nobody here seems to care about how chaotic a work environment we're in. They're just rushing ahead with things.* His train of thought was interrupted by the sight of Howard coming toward him. *Great,* Ray thought. *What does he want now?*

"Ray. Question. There's a glitch on one of the screens in the app. Did you review the code yet?

"No, I simply haven't had time."

"Okay. Well, what do you think it could be?"

"Nothing good. Everything's falling apart."

Howard was taken aback. *Where is all the negativity coming from?*

WHAT'S GOING ON HERE

Ray Phillips wants everything to be perfect—and that's a great quality in a software engineer. But he can get into the habit of only looking for what's wrong and start saying "No" to everything.

When he does this, he is seen to be negative by those around him even if he's only trying to make sure that quality (measured by his standards) is delivered.

LET'S TRY THAT AGAIN

Howard Dunn, the Chief Technology Officer for 366 Solar, was reviewing the performance of their new app.

The soon to launch application would keep track of the energy expenditure of each customer's solar array and use the mobile phone's camera to measure the intensity of the sunlight to calculate how much power each panel could generate.

He had held off on releasing it because of the Alta California bid. Now that they were well underway with that project, he was supervising putting the app through the final testing phase.

Everything looks good, he thought. He was glad he had listened to Emily Reed. She had been right about not launching earlier. Since then, he had uncovered some flaws that, while not fatal, would have detracted from the user's experience. Which was exactly what Emily had stressed. *I'm glad she found a way to get through my tunnel vision.*

As he ran the app through its final benchmark, he noticed a glitch on one of the screens. *Hmm,* he thought. *That won't look good. And Emily will not be happy either.* He stood up and headed over to see his group of engineers about the issue.

Ray Phillips was one of those engineers. Since the Alta California deal had gone through, he had been brought on board to help with the programming load. He had been working on the application full time for weeks, including staying late and working weekends.

Even with all of the extra time, he wasn't happy about the situation. The quality of the work being done was simply not up to what he considered to be the proper standard. *Nobody here seems to care about how chaotic a work environment we're in. They're just rushing ahead with things.* His train of thought was interrupted by the sight of Howard coming toward him. *Great,* Ray thought. *What does he want now?*

"Ray. Question. There's a glitch on one of the screens in the app. Did you review the code yet?

"No, I simply haven't had time."

"Okay. Well, what do you think it could be?"

"Nothing good. Everything's falling apart"

Howard was taken aback. *Where is all the negativity coming from?*

"I realize that. Could it be an issue with the compiler?"

"What makes you think it could be that? We ran it more than enough times to know there should be no glitches."

"Boot it and walk me through it."

Ray let out a deep sigh. "If there's a bug, it's going to take the whole team. Do you really think just the two of us will find it?"

Again with the negativity. He's just looking for any excuse to say 'no'. Howard realized that Ray's attitude was detrimental to the team. But he did have talent, so maybe there was a better way of letting him know his behavior wasn't acceptable.

"That doesn't matter. We'll always come up with issues. But if we only focus on what's wrong, we'll miss obvious answers. I appreciate your ability to point out problems, but it won't help to solve the issue."

Ray considered that for a second. *He could be right. But I'm not convinced it will be so easy.* "These things are never that simple, Howard. But I guess we can try."

Howard smiled and rubbed his hands together. "Let's dig into that code."

If he can keep such a positive attitude, Ray thought. *I guess it wouldn't hurt to follow in his footsteps.*

HOW TO BE MOST EFFECTIVE WITH A NAYSAYER

Howard managed to curb Ray's bad behavior by diverting his negative attitude into a search for a positive solution.

He stressed that the behavior wasn't good for the company or the workplace while still recognizing Ray's positive motivation in saying "No."

- Your goal is to carefully move them from problems to solutions.
- Listen attentively to what they have to say so that they know they have been heard.
- If possible, acknowledge that they have good intentions. This doesn't mean that you should agree with them. Don't follow your acknowledgement with the word "but."
- Ask questions that begin with the words "what" or "how" to get them to focus on the solution rather than the problem.

THE TIME BOMB

The motivation for this difficult behavior can be either People or Action.

And since the motivation has moved toward the extreme, it has shifted from focusing on People into seeking Attention or from Action into Control.

Time Bombs will have rapid mood swings. Any situation that seems out of control will set them off into emotional outbursts.

MEET THE PEOPLE

Name	Role	Communication Style	Motivation
Paul Morgan	CEO	Doer	Action
Stacy O'Sullivan	Chief Operating Officer	Solver	Order
Oscar Brown	Corporate Counsel	Persuader	People, Action

The conference call had barely ended when Oscar Brown burst into the conference room.

Uh, oh, Stacy thought. *What now?*

They had just finished with one problem and it looked like another storm was brewing on the horizon. *No, scratch that.* From the look on Oscar's face, it looked like the storm was about to burst upon them.

Oscar was the corporate counsel for 366 Solar. They had brought him on board during the Alta California deal. Before that, they had used an outside firm to handle all their legal matters. However, Paul had decided to hire someone full time to manage all of the details for them.

Stacy had never been too happy with the hire. While he was a smart lawyer who had the gift of gab, he also seemed somewhat volatile to Stacy. In previous interactions, she had noticed there was no middle ground with him. He went from 0 to 60 in a flash.

For his part, Oscar Brown was not too happy, either.

I can't believe they're doing this to me, he thought as he prepared to deliver the news to Paul and Stacy. *This better be fixed. And fast.* He considered sitting down but thought he'd have more of their attention if he stayed standing.

"Have you not read your emails?"

And that's the textbook definition of how not to start a conversation, Stacy thought. *I wonder how Paul is going to react?*

"Not yet," Paul replied. "What's going on?"

"I just got an email from the President of Alta California. Turns out, he wants to revise some of the language of the contract." Oscar started pacing in front of them.

Paul saw it as a problem to be solved. He nodded. "Okay. What does he want?"

Oscar threw his hands up in frustration. "Why does that even matter? It's not what he wants. It's the simple fact that he wants it! Do you have any idea how hard I worked on this?"

Stacy realized the situation was going downhill fast. They had to do something before Oscar went ballistic.

WHAT'S GOING ON HERE

Oscar sees the changes in the contract as a personal attack on him and a block to completing the deal. When the rest of the team doesn't seem to understand the severity of the problem, he prepares to detonate to focus their attention on him and the problem.

What can Paul and Stacy do to help Oscar curb his bad behavior?

LET'S TRY THAT AGAIN

The conference call had barely ended when Oscar Brown burst into the conference room.

Uh. oh, Stacy thought. *What now?*

They had just finished with one problem and it looked like another storm was brewing on the horizon. *No, scratch that.* From the look on Oscar's face, it looked like the storm was about to burst upon them.

Oscar was the corporate counsel for 366 Solar. They had brought him on board during the Alta California deal. Before that, they had used an outside firm to handle all their legal matters. However, Paul had decided to hire someone full time to manage all of the details for them.

Stacy had never been too happy with the hire. While he was a smart lawyer who had the gift of gab, he also seemed somewhat volatile to Stacy. In previous interactions, she had noticed there was no middle ground with him. He went from 0 to 60 in a flash.

For his part, Oscar Brown was not too happy, either.

I can't believe they're doing this to me, he thought as he prepared to deliver the news to Paul and Stacy. *This better be fixed. And fast.* He considered sitting down but thought he'd have more of their attention if he stayed standing.

"Have you not read your emails?"

And that's the textbook definition of how not to start a conversation, Stacy thought. *I wonder how Paul is going to react?*

"Not yet," Paul replied. "What's going on?"

"I just got an email from the President of Alta California. Turns out, he wants to revise some of the language of the contract." Oscar started pacing in front of them.

Paul saw it as a problem to be solved. He nodded. "Okay. What does he want?"

Oscar threw his hands up in frustration. "Why does that even matter? It's not what he wants. It's the simple fact that he wants it! Do you have any idea how hard I worked on this?"

Stacy realized the situation was going downhill fast. They had to do something before Oscar went ballistic.

Paul took immediate stock of the situation. It was obvious Oscar wasn't happy. *Well, that's actually an understatement.*

His first instinct was to berate him for entering uninvited into the conference room. And he definitely did not like the tone he was using. It was detrimental to the situation at hand and if anybody outside heard it, it would set a bad precedent for acceptable behavior at 366 Solar. Instead, Paul thought back to how Danielle had handled their situation with Michael over the phone. He decided to moderate his approach. Going head-to-head with Oscar might result in both of them letting their emotions take over.

"Oscar. What was in the email?"

"Huh?" Oscar replied. *Why does he care about the email? Did he not hear me when I said they wanted to change the terms of the contract? I can't believe this!* "There are over a hundred pages in this contract. It's ridiculous. Unprofessional!"

Stacy saw Oscar was going to continue to rant. She looked over at Paul and wondered if she should step in. He saw her look and shook his head.

"Oscar. I understand your frustration. Let's look at how we can handle your situation.

Finally! Oscar thought. *Some appreciation for what they're putting me through.* He stopped pacing to address Paul. "Yes. I'm upset. Although that may not be a strong enough word to describe it."

"What are your concerns?"

"Well, for starters, any changes in the contract involves the consent of so many people. I'm not sure the President understands that. They're a state university. And we're using federal funds as well."

"I understand. Is that everything?"

"Of course not! It's also about the revisions. They want to involve the engineering students and faculty on the project."

Paul nodded. "I see. Anything else?"

"I think that's enough. Don't you?"

Paul thought about the situation.

The deal with Alta California was a big thing for 366 Solar. The changes in the contract didn't seem like something for Oscar to be so concerned about. And certainly not worthy of that blow-up. It seemed to Paul that he made the situation much more dramatic than it needed to be.

"I will address these issues directly with the President of Alta California," Paul said.

"You will?" Oscar asked. "Well, good. Yes. That's how they should be dealt with. Personally." Oscar felt the anger draining from him. Paul had managed to deal with his concerns while not taking away any importance from them.

I've never been treated like that, Oscar thought. *He understands what I want.*

"Do you have any other concerns Oscar?"

He really is attentive. A good leader. "Not right now. No." Oscar thought about his outburst. About how he had handled the situation. It had angered him so much that he had just leapt from his desk and went straight to find Paul. *That may not have been the best way to handle this.*

"Very well," Paul said. "I'll take the matter into my own hands."

Oscar nodded. "Thank you Paul. I...I appreciate it." That had been hard to say, but he felt it was necessary.

After the outburst, Paul wasn't expecting that type of response from Oscar. *Maybe he learned from whole situation.* "You're welcome, Oscar. I'll keep you posted on what happens."

"Thank you." Oscar smiled and left the conference room.

Stacy chuckled. "Two crises in a row? What else is going to happen today?"

Paul laughed along with Stacy. "I think that's enough. For today at least."

HOW TO BE MOST EFFECTIVE WITH A TIME BOMB

Here are some tips about how to be more effective when dealing with a Time Bomb:

- Repeat their name as a pattern interrupt just like you would with a Bully. This will help to drain their emotion so they can express themselves in a more rational way and you can understand what the problem really is.
- After they've told you the problem, make sure that you have it all by asking if there's more. Keep going until all the emotion has been drained and they regain control.

THE SILENT TYPE

The motivation of the silent type is rooted in Order and Safety. When taken to an extreme, this type of person will go silent and stop talking. They won't respond to emails or texts and will try to hide.

Their strategy to deal with the stress of the problem— their way of keeping safe—is to simply avoid contact with the situation.

MEET THE PEOPLE

Name	Role	Communication Style	Motivation
Emily Reed	Chief Experience Officer	Supporter	Safety
Danielle Edmonds	Executive Assistant	Blend	
Gary Peters	Network Administrator	Analyzer	Safety

Danielle Edmonds almost cried out. *Not again!* she thought. *It's the third time this week. How am I supposed to get anything done?*

The internet was down yet again. Her inbox was packed with emails and she couldn't afford to fall behind. The mere thought of not replying to people sent shudders down her spine. She could use her phone, but it would take forever.

It was her responsibility to keep everybody aware of what was happening. And she couldn't do her job with her hands tied behind her back. *That's exactly what it feels like to work without internet,* she realized. *What is going on in the IT department?*

Danielle had sent several emails to the network administrator, Gary Peters. It had always been hard trying to get a direct answer from him and it always took him longer than normal to respond to any email.

He wasn't a very talkative person, either, and tended to almost disappear into the background. When he did manage to speak up everyone was always surprised.

His response to her emails had been a vague commitment to "look into it." *Well,* she thought, *I don't think he's looking hard enough.* With a sigh, Danielle pushed back her chair and stood up. It was time to go see about this issue in person.

She wasn't alone in her frustration. Emily Reed was having the same issues. She was tired of the internet being down. She had called Gary twice already, but her call had gone straight to voicemail. *Something needs to be done,* she thought. *This can't continue. I can't be the only one who's having issues.*

Gary Peters could attest to the fact that she wasn't the only one. His phone had been ringing constantly. Each time he picked up it was the same issue—the internet, but there was nothing he could do to fix it. *What more can I do?* The pressure had started to get to him. So much so that he stopped replying to emails or answering his phone. The constant demands on his attention had frazzled him and he found it easier to isolate himself in order to focus.

The stillness he was trying to create was shattered by the sound of Danielle Edmond's voice. "Gary, it's Danielle. Do you have a minute?"

He struggled to respond. "Yes." *What am I going to say to her?*

Danielle let herself into the office. She found Gary sitting in his chair against the far wall of the office. "There you are!" Gary just nodded in response.

Danielle approached him. "I'm sure you're aware of the problem we've been having with the internet. Any luck?"

Gary shook his head.

Why doesn't he answer me? Danielle thought. She knew he had a strange reputation, but he had always been efficient at his job. *What's going on?*

Danielle was about to say something else when Emily Reed came into the office.

Gary's eyes widened at the sight of her. *Oh, no,* he thought.

Emily wasn't surprised to find Danielle there already. *She's always so on top of things.* "Danielle! Good to see you! I don't have to guess why you're here."

She turned to Gary. "What's going on? It's the third time this week the internet's been down."

He didn't reply to her question. *That's odd,* she thought. "Gary? Gary! Anything?" She looked over at Danielle. "Did he say anything to you?"

"Nothing."

Emily shook her head. "What's going on?"

She didn't know it, but Danielle had just asked herself the exact same question.

WHAT'S GOING ON HERE

The Silent Type does not respond well to pressure. When pressure builds or they are forced to make a decision, they "go silent."

How can Danielle get the answers she needs from Gary without having him fall further into his bad behavior?

LET'S TRY THAT AGAIN

Danielle Edmonds almost cried out. *Not again!* she thought. *It's the third time this week. How am I supposed to get anything done?* The internet was down yet again. Her inbox was packed with emails and she couldn't afford to fall behind. The mere thought of not replying to people sent shudders down her spine. She could use her phone, but it would take forever.

It was her responsibility to keep everybody aware of what was happening. And she couldn't do her job with her hands tied behind her back. *That's exactly what it feels like to work without internet,* she realized. *What is going on in the IT department?*

Danielle had sent several emails to the network administrator, Gary Peters. It had always been hard trying to get a direct answer from him and it always took him longer than normal to respond to any email. He wasn't a very talkative person, either, and tended to almost disappear into the background. When he did manage to speak up, everyone was always surprised.

His response to her emails had been a vague commitment to "look into it." *Well,* she thought, *I don't think he's looking hard enough.* With a sigh, Danielle pushed back her chair and stood up. It was time to go see about this issue in person.

She wasn't alone in her frustration. Emily Reed was having the same issues. She was tired of the internet being down. She had called Gary twice already, but her call had gone straight to voicemail. *Something needs to be done,* she thought. *This can't continue. I can't be the only one who's having issues.*

Gary Peters could attest to the fact that she wasn't the only one. His phone had been ringing constantly. Each time he picked up it was the same issue—the internet, but there was nothing he could do to fix it. *What more can I do?* The pressure had started to get to him. So much so that he stopped replying to emails or answering his phone. The constant demands on his attention had frazzled him and he found it easier to isolate himself in order to focus.

The stillness he was trying to create was shattered by the sound of Danielle Edmond's voice. "Gary, it's Danielle. Do you have a minute?"

He struggled to respond. "Yes." *What am I going to say to her?*

Danielle let herself into the office. She found Gary sitting in his chair against the far wall of the office. "There you are!" Gary just nodded in response.

Danielle approached him. "I'm sure you're aware of the problem we've been having with the internet. Any luck?"

Gary shook his head.

Why doesn't he answer me? Danielle thought. She knew he had a strange reputation, but he had always been efficient at his job. *What's going on?*

Danielle was about to say something else when Emily Reed came into the office.

Gary's eyes widened at the sight of her. *Oh, no,* he thought.

Emily wasn't surprised to find Danielle there already. *She's always so on top of things.* "Danielle! Good to see you! I don't have to guess why you're here."

She turned to Gary. "What's going on? It's the third time this week the internet's been down."

He didn't reply to her question. *That's odd,* she thought. "Gary? Gary! Anything?" She looked over at Danielle. "Did he say anything to you?"

"Nothing."

Emily shook her head. "What's going on?"

She didn't know it but Danielle had just asked herself the exact same question. *Not only is he not answering his emails, he's not even talking to us.*

Emily walked toward Gary "I'm sure you're aware of the problem. Something needs to be done."

Gary heard her but he found he couldn't respond. The pressure from not knowing how to solve the problem kept him frozen in place.

Danielle realized that pressuring Gary might be the wrong thing to do. She knew he took a long time to reply to emails. Maybe they just had to provide him with more space to respond.

Danielle cleared her throat "Do you have any idea what the problem may be?" Her question floated on the air between them. The silence stretched for so long that Danielle didn't know whether to prod him further or ask something else. Emily opened her mouth to say something, but Danielle raised her finger, asking her to wait. *Just give him time,* she thought.

Gary looked at the both of them. "Yes. I...I think it's on the provider's end."

Well, why didn't you say so in the first place?! Emily thought. She shook her head and was about to say something else when Danielle beat her to it. "What have you done to approach them?" *I have to keep drawing him out,* she thought to herself. She only hoped that Emily would recognize what she was doing and follow suit.

There was another long silence after her question.

"I emailed them," Gary said. "There seems to be new construction. An exit ramp off the highway. It's disrupting everything."

It dawned on Emily what Danielle was doing. She was giving him room to talk. It wasn't *her* preferred way to handle things but it was better than his silence.

We're getting closer, Danielle thought. "Do they know when they'll have it back? We can't work with faulty internet connections." More silence followed this question. It stretched on even further than the previous ones. She was about to say something when Gary spoke up once more.

"Tomorrow. They're sending someone tomorrow."

Danielle sighed. *That was almost like pulling teeth.* "Thank you, Gary. I'll let everybody know." Gary just nodded in response again.

She handled that great, Emily thought. *She really is the ambassador around here.* "I appreciate the information, Gary." She spun on her heel and strode with Danielle out of the office.

Gary breathed a sigh of relief. *That didn't go as bad as I thought it would. Not as stressful.* He was thankful that Danielle had given him the space he needed to feel comfortable.

Meanwhile, out in the hallway, Emily and Danielle had stopped to discuss what had just happened.

"That was a real test of patience," Emily said. "I don't know how you do it."

"Well, we do what we have to in order to understand and be understood."

"True. But do you ever find it to be too much?"

Danielle thought about her answer. "It can be taxing sometimes. But I've always believed that good communication is the bedrock of any successful enterprise. And that the result of every communication is *my* responsibility. I just have to be flexible enough."

Emily smiled. "I like that. It should be your motto."

"Maybe," Danielle replied. "Just maybe."

HOW TO BE MOST EFFECTIVE WITH THE SILENT TYPE

Danielle had to draw Gary out in order to get the information she needed. By not challenging him directly and using open-ended questions, she was able to break through his bad behavior.

When working with a Silent Type, ask your question, then be quiet and let them answer you. No matter how long it takes. We tend to see silence as bad thing, as a void that needs to be filled, but in this type of situation you have to be willing to outwait the Silent Type.

- Use open-ended questions to draw them out, but don't badger them with a series of questions as that will only cause them to withdraw more.]
- Use body language that lets them know you aren't condemning or criticizing them.
- Wait attentively and patiently as long you possibly can for them to say something. They'll get the idea you aren't going to talk and fill the silence.
- If all else fails, terminate the conversation and tell them what you are going to do. This probably won't make them say anything, but it will move you toward action.

THE WHINER

The Whiner is motivated both by the need for Order and the need for Safety. In an effort to keep things logical and orderly, they find themselves constantly looking for faults and this results in their complaining about things.

This pursuit of order and perfection can be taken to an extreme where they complain about everything because they feel they lack the power to do anything about it.

MEET THE PEOPLE

Name	Role	Communication Style	Motivation
Tyler Hughes	Chief Financial Officer	Analyzer	Order
Chad Cole	Insurance Advisor	Perfectionist	Order

Tyler thought about his earlier meeting with Russell Davis.

It had been a close call. He had almost quit. *I still don't know how Paul manages him,* he thought. Russell had always been a difficult person. Tyler was amazed at how he had managed to calm the man down and still get his point across. It was a lesson he would store for future interactions. *Just not in the immediate future,* he thought wryly.

Tyler booted up his computer, shifting his thoughts toward the matter at hand. He had gotten a request for a Skype meeting with Chad Cole, the outside insurance advisor for 366 Solar. They had worked with him on the Alta California deal and, while he tended to be somewhat of a downer, Tyler had empathized with his outlook. He was a stickler for details himself and could definitely relate. *I wonder what he wants to discuss, though,* Tyler thought as he opened the Skype application.

On the other end, Chad Cole was carefully constructing his arguments. He wasn't happy about the school construction project 366 Solar had decided to take on. The deal with Alta California had given him enough headaches. *Why did they even get involved? I don't think they're aware of all of the potential downfalls. There's too much liability for them.* Chad hit connect on Skype and waited for Tyler to answer.

Tyler replied to the request and Chad's face filled the screen. "Hey, Chad."

"Hello, Tyler. How's it going?"

"Not bad. You wanted to talk to me about something?"

Chad took a deep breath. "Yeah. I don't like the school project. I really don't. It's too complicated. Too many factors involved."

Well, that's a terrible way to start off a meeting, Tyler thought. They had barely begun talking and Chad was already telling him what was wrong. *I wonder if that's what I sound like sometimes?* "We really want to go through with this."

Chad shook his head. "It exposes the company. There's too much liability involved. I don't think we can get you coverage. Have you even run this past the shareholders? Does it have their approval?"

Tyler realized the questions were going to come nonstop. How was he going to head them off?

WHAT'S GOING ON HERE

As an insurance advisor, Chad sees it as his job to find the potential problems and risk in everything. The problems is that he never gives any thought to how he presents the problems to other people.

LET'S TRY THAT AGAIN

Tyler thought about his earlier meeting with Russell Davis.

It had been a close call. He had almost quit. *I still don't know how Paul manages him*, he thought. Russell had always been a difficult person. Tyler was amazed at how he had managed to calm the man down and still get his point across. It was a lesson he would store for future interactions. *Just not in the immediate future,* he thought wryly.

Tyler booted up his computer, shifting his thoughts toward the matter at hand. He had gotten a request for a Skype meeting with Chad Cole, the outside insurance advisor for 366 Solar. They had worked with him on the Alta California deal and, while he tended to be somewhat of a downer, Tyler had empathized with his outlook. He was a stickler for details himself and could definitely relate. *I wonder what he wants to discuss, though,* Tyler thought as he opened the Skype application.

On the other end, Chad Cole was carefully constructing his arguments. He wasn't happy about the school construction project 366 Solar had decided to take on. The deal with Alta California had given him enough headaches. *Why did they even get involved? I don't think they're aware of all of the potential downfalls. There's too much liability for them.* Chad hit connect on Skype and waited for Tyler to answer.

Tyler replied to the request and Chad's face filled the screen. "Hey, Chad."

"Hello, Tyler. How's it going?"

"Not bad. You wanted to talk to me about something?

Chad took a deep breath. "Yeah. I don't like the school project. I really don't. It's too complicated. Too many factors involved."

Well, that's a terrible way to start off a meeting, Tyler thought. They had barely begun talking and Chad was already telling him about what was wrong. *I wonder if that's what I sound like sometimes?* "We really want to go through with this."

Chad shook his head. "It exposes the company. There's too much liability involved. I don't think we can get you coverage. Have you even run this past the shareholders? Does it have their approval?"

Tyler realized the questions were going to come nonstop. How was he going to head them off?

I don't think I can. He thought back to his meeting with Russell Davis. *Nor should I. Had I confronted Russell it would have been bad for everyone. But with Chad, I think the best thing is to face each of his objections head on.*

He understood where Chad was coming from. He also tended to question everything. *But never with this level of negativity,* he thought. So, *what can I do to help him along?* "Yes," Tyler said. "We ran it past the shareholders. They're all on board. And eager, too, I might add."

Oh, thought Chad. *But I still don't like it.* "There's more liability coverage. Children at the school. Parents. It's going to cost more."

Paul had approved the budget. "I appreciate that you bring up the question of money. But we have the budget for it."

Maybe they do know what they're getting into, Chad thought. "Vehicle insurance. Did you think of that? They pick up and drop off kids."

Now there's a legitimate concern, Tyler thought. "I'm glad you brought that up. Right now I can say, yes, we're on board with that.

See? They don't know everything. Chad decided to press forward "Property and equipment and—"

"Yes, I'm aware of all of that." Tyler said. He had interrupted Chad because he was starting to go off the rails. He had to put a stop to it right now. "It's nothing we haven't done before there."

"I just want you to be aware of everything."

"I understand."

"Directors and officer's insurance. You know, in case the directors and officers are sued for any related risks."

"We already have that."

Tyler then realized that it wasn't just about facing his objections. He had to instill some confidence in Chad if he was going to move forward. "I appreciate your concerns, Chad. It keeps us on our toes. How about we do this? Why don't you send me a document with all of your doubts and questions? I'll make sure they're expressed to the board and to Paul as well."

Tyler's suggestion served as a balm for Chad's troubled soul. *Maybe I don't have to worry so much. They seem to have things under control.* "I can do that."

Tyler smiled. "Perfect. Please let me know if anything else comes up."

Chad thought about his interaction with Tyler. It had gone a lot better than he had thought it would. *He's a good example to follow.* "I definitely will. Good-bye Tyler."

"Good-bye."

Tyler hit 'end' on the virtual call. He chuckled to himself. *That went much better than with Russell Davis. I guess I must be learning.*

HOW TO BE MOST EFFECTIVE WITH A WHINER

Tyler managed to curb Chad's difficult behavior by satisfying his constant doubts. Instead of ignoring or belittling him, he made him feel secure in the knowledge that his complaints would be addressed to in the proper manner.

Tyler's strategy made Chad feel safe as well as satisfying his need for order, the motivations which had caused him to start complaining in the beginning.

- If they are a constant whiner, listen to them and acknowledge what they are saying, but don't agree with them even if you think they might be right as this will just encourage more complaining.
- If they whine about another person, ask them if they have voiced their complaint to that other person. They probably haven't, so ask them if it's OK for you to tell the other person what they said. They'll get the idea and stop complaining to you about other people.
- Don't argue or use logic because you will never win. Acknowledge what they are saying then use the word "but" and ask them a question that gets them to think about a solution or an alternative to what they are whining about.

Your Action Plan

Now what?

If you've read (or even skimmed) to this part of the book, congratulations!

You've done something most people will never do—learn how to be a more effective communicator in any situation. Quite an accomplishment!

Over the years of working with my private clients, students, and corporations I've realized that the biggest challenge faced by most people is implementation. How do you actually use what you've learned?

People read the book, attend the event, study the material, and probably even practice it before they leave but when the pressure of real life intervenes they revert to their old habits and patterns. It's quite natural.

It doesn't make them failures or bad people, it's just reality. You can't instantly undo ten, twenty, thirty, forty, or more years of habits simply by reading a book.

It's a great start and many people get "ah ha" moments that create instant change as they read. They "get it" and put it to use right away. But most readers need an action plan.

THE BEST APPROACH

In my experience, trying to implement everything at once is the biggest cause of frustration. Most of what you have learned is new and it can easily be overwhelming.

The best approach is to break what you have learned and want to accomplish into a series of small steps, then practice each step before you move on to the next one. You don't have to achieve perfection with each step, just taking action is enough for most people.

THE SECRET POWER OF ACTION

One thing that will have a big impact on your success as a communicator is this: TAKE ACTION NOW. Do something right away before habit and inertia set in.

But what action to take?

Investing ten minutes in using these pages to create your personal action plan will get you started and keep you moving on your journey to communication excellence.

So...let's quit talking and get started!

YOUR ACTION PLANNER

- Commit now to taking ten minutes to complete your plan.
- Complete all of the parts.
- I've included some space for answers here, but you might want to use another sheet of paper or word processor.

YOUR OUTCOME

What will be the benefits of becoming a better communicator?

What will happen or continue to happen if you don't improve? Negative motivation can be very powerful, so don't skip this.

KNOW YOURSELF

What is your Communication Style? _____

Are you more task or people oriented in your Style?

Are you more big picture or detail oriented in your Style?

How does using this Style serve you well?

In what situations or with which people does your Style limit you or cause you problems?

THOSE AROUND YOU

List four people you interact with on a regular basis, what you think their style is, and how you can be more effective with each of them. Remember: *Step Up, Not Down!*

PERSON #1

Their Name   _____

Their Style   _____

How can you be more effective with this person?

PERSON #2

Their Name   _____

Their Style   _____

How can you be more effective with this person?

PERSON #3

Their Name   _____

Their Style   _____

How can you be more effective with this person?

PERSON #4

Their Name   _____

Their Style   _____

How can you be more effective with this person?

GET SPECIFIC

What is the one thing you will commit to doing immediately?

When will you start?

Where will you practice?

How will you measure your progress?

How will you reward yourself?

What do you want to tell yourself?

ACTION CURES FEAR - TAKE ACTION NOW
Share your story at
www.facebook.com/communicationstyles2

I look forward to seeing you at a live event!

Fifteen Years in Five Minutes

It's taken me fifteen years of research and working with tens of thousands of people to create the *Communication Styles 2.0* model, but I know that some of the Styles who read this (the action/big picture styles) just want a summary. So here it is in three bullet points:

- Everyone has a natural Communication Style which is a person's regular or familiar communication patterns and the strategies they use to communicate across a broad variety of situations. It's how we relate to others.
- There are two dimensions of communication and everyone falls somewhere on these two axis:

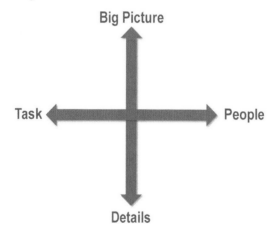

- To be a successful communicator, understand where you fall on each of the axis and where the other person falls. Be aware of your natural tendencies and adapt them to match the Style of the other person.

You can find out more at www.communicationstyles2.com

Find Your Exact Communication Style Now!

Use the new *Communication Styles 2.0* online survey to uncover your natural communication tendencies and get your Personal Insight Report in less than ten minutes.

You'll get a customized report that you and everyone in your group can use to understand each other and get fast improvement - even if you have been communication challenged in the past.

Based on the proven *Communication Styles 2.0* model, your easy-to-read report delivers insights and actionable advice that you can put to use immediately.

- Your exact communication style and tendencies
- Fast overview and details to match your style
- Your strengths and how to take advantage of them
- Your challenges and a customized action plan
- How you can be most effective with each of the other styles
- How others can be more effective with you
- Optional team maps for fast insight
- Customized live and online training available

www.communicationstyles2.com/survey

Made in the USA
Middletown, DE
28 August 2019